Pictorial History of
the Mediterranean Air War

Pictorial History of the Mediterranean Air War

Volume 1: RAF 1940–43

Christopher F. Shores

LONDON
IAN ALLAN

First Published 1972

ISBN: 0 7110 0382 3

Published by Ian Allan Ltd, Shepperton, Surrey and
printed in Great Britain by Cox and Wyman Ltd, London, Fakenham and Reading.

Contents

Introduction

From tiny beginnings the Royal Air Force in the Mediterranean areas based as it was in June 1940 in Egypt and Palestine, was to grow in a period of three years to become a mighty force which was to play a major part in the defeat of Germany and Italy in Southern Europe.

It was a long and hard battle, for despite the achievement of numerical superiority quite early in the conflict, it was to be considerably longer before qualitative superiority was to follow. As a consequence, during much of the period covered by this first volume, the losses suffered during the exercise of a steadily-improving standard of close support to the armies on the ground, were at times severe to say the least.

Many factors affected this struggle for supremacy in the air – the wide dispersion of available forces at times of crisis – Malta, Greece, Crete, Iraq, Syria, etc.; the entry of Japan into the war at the critical phase of Operation 'Crusader' in the Libyan Desert; the early Allied victory in Italian East Africa, releasing growing numbers of squadrons of the South African Air Force for service further north; and the direct delivery of substantial numbers of aircraft from the United States of America.

During the years when no invasion of North-Western Europe could be seriously considered, the Mediterranean was the one area where something could be done by the British and Commonwealth forces, gaining combat experience, protecting vital links with Middle East oil supplies, and with India and the East, drawing substantial Axis forces away from the great battlefields of the Eastern Front in Russia, and eventually effectively threatening the 'soft underbelly of Europe' – a threat that was ultimately to become an actuality.

The Royal Air Force learned much in the Mediterranean that was later put to good use during the invasion of Normandy, and over the steaming jungles of Burma; for the British it was the birthplace of true ground support operations in World War II.

March 1972.   C. F. S.

The Outbreak of War in the Mediterranean

The Mediterranean is an area of very great strategic importance to the countries of the Western world, a fact which the events of the twentieth century have so far done little to disprove. Situated between the continents of Europe and Africa, it offers not only seaboards to the countries surrounding it, but also easy access to Asia, via the Black Sea, and to the Far East, via the Suez Canal. To add to this is the vital factor of oil; although today Libya is an important producer of oil, this was not the case until recently, but Syria provides port facilities to pipelines from deep in Iraq, and the Suez Canal offers access to the oil-rich territories of Iran and the Arabian Gulf.

The only natural entry to the Mediterranean is through the Straits of Gibraltar from the Atlantic in the west, and a number of islands, noteably Malta, Crete and Cyprus, provide bases from which control over large areas of the sea can be exercised. In 1939, when France and the United Kingdom became embroiled in war with Hitler's Germany, the only real threat to their security in this area was from Italy, where Mussolini, the Fascist dictator, waited to see what course events would indicate as offering the greatest advantage to his country before he made a move. At this stage Spain, although in sympathy with the totalitarian regimes, lay exhausted from her long and bloody civil war, which had ended only a few months earlier; besides this, in order to reach her frontiers, the Germans or Italians must first pass through France – still nominally the great bastion of Free Europe at that time.

Thus from the west, the entry to the Mediterranean was controlled by the British fortress base of Gibraltar; the south of France and the French North African colonies gave easy control of most of the Western Mediterranean, aided by the French island of Corsica. Then in the centre came the Italian domain, Italy on the north coast extending far southwards to divide the Mediterranean virtually into two basins. Opposite lay her colony of Libya, a land of barren deserts stretching deep into the Sahara. Between these two, however, lay the island of Malta, long a British naval base. Beyond Italy lay Albania, which she had recently occupied, and then the neutral Balkans – Yugoslavia, Greece and Turkey. The rest of the coast, from the Turkish border at the eastern end, to the Libyan border, was all in Allied hands; Syria, controlled by the French, Palestine and Egypt, together with the vital Suez Canal, controlled by the British.

Against such a background, the Mediterranean seemed relatively secure, and with defences at home under strength and an expeditionary force in France to maintain, the British forces in this area enjoyed a relatively low priority. By the spring of 1940 a small but efficient air force, Royal Air Force Middle East, was based mainly in the south-east corner of the area. In Egypt, for the defence of the Suez Canal zone and the port of Alexandria, an important naval base, was 202 Group, commanded by Air Commodore Raymond Collishaw. This Group comprised three squadrons of Gloster Gladiator fighter biplanes, 33, 80 and 112; a single Hawker Hurricane 1 monoplane fighter was also available, serving with 80 Squadron; four squadrons of Bristol Blenheim 1 bombers, 30, 45, 55 and 211, and one squadron of Blenheim 4s, 113; one army co-operation squadron with Westland Lysanders, 208; there were also two squadrons of bomber-transports, 216 with Bristol Bombays and 70 with Vickers Valentias.

To the east were more units; 6 Squadron with Lysanders and Gladia-tors was in Palestine for army co-operation, while in Iraq were 84 Squadron with Blenheim 1s and 244 Squadron with Vickers Vincent general purpose biplanes. On Malta were no squadrons as such, but twelve Royal Navy Sea Gladiators were available in crates, having been brought to the island as replacements for the aircraft carriers operating in the area. Now by special arrangement, some of these were released to the RAF, and four were erected during April to form a Fighter Flight at Hal Far airfield to provide a makeshift defence for the island. Finally, based at Gibraltar, and operating over both the Mediterranean and the Atlantic, was 202 Squadron with Saro London biplane flying-boats.

RAF Middle East also disposed one and a half squadrons in Aden with Blenheim 1s, Gladiators and Vincents, and three squadrons of Vickers Wellesley bombers in the Sudan, but operations of these units were outside the area of the Mediterranean and are not dealt with here.

On May 10th, 1940, the great German 'Blitzkrieg' was launched in Western Europe, and France quickly crumbled. Seizing his opportunity to partake of the spoils of what seemed imminent German victory, Mussolini declared war on the Allies on the evening of June 10th and at once invaded Southern France. At one fell swoop the whole situation in the Mediterranean area had changed radically, and much to the disadvantage of the British; the collapse of France seemed imminent, and without the support of French arms, the British forces were greatly outnumbered. In Libya alone the Regia Aeronautica enjoyed a three to one superiority in aircraft on hand over the RAF in Egypt, and elsewhere the ratio was even greater.

Despite this numerical inferiority, the RAF responded at once in keeping with its doctrine of attack being the best form of defence, and in the early morning of June 11th, 26 Blenheims from 45, 55 and 113 Squadrons attacked the Italian airfield at El Adem, destroying a number of aircraft on the ground. Anti-aircraft fire was heavy and fighters were up, two Blenheims failing to return and a third crash-landing at Sidi Barrani. On this same day the Italians despatched two formations of bombers, escorted by fighters, to bomb Valetta harbour and airfields on Malta; two Fighter Flight Sea Gladiators intercepted, claiming one of the attackers shot down.

The early opposition by Italian fighters over Libya led to the immediate despatch of a flight of Gladiators from 33 Squadron forward to Sidi Barrani for bomber-escort duties, and to patrol over the front. At the same time British patrols moved across the border and captured two Italian frontier forts.

An attempt was made to provide some reinforcements while the route across France was still open, three Hurricanes arriving on June 13th and being allocated to 80 Squadron. Six more were to stage through Malta a week later, leaving behind one of their number which had crashed on landing. Meanwhile, on June 14th the Gladiators of 33 Squadron engaged in their first combat over Fort Capuzzo, attacking a Caproni Ca 310 and escorting Fiat CR 32 fighters, claiming the bomber and one of the fighters shot down, with one more probably destroyed for no loss.

Thereafter air activity over the front increased, and on the 17th the Gladiators at Sidi Barrani were reinforced by the arrival of one Hurricane from 80 Squadron, and two fighter Blenheim 1Fs of 30 Squadron; on the outbreak of war this latter unit had at once converted its aircraft to the fighter role by the addition of under-fuselage packs carrying four forward-firing machine-guns. Two days later four Gladiators and the

Hurricane became involved with a number of Italian CR 42 fighters while on patrol, claiming four shot down, two by the Hurricane, for the loss of one Gladiator.

During the night of June 21st–22nd Alexandria suffered its first air raid, and on the 24th the Franco/Italian armistice was signed, leaving the British alone both in Western Europe and the Mediterranean to face the combined military might of the Axis partners. Malta had by this time suffered a few more desultory air raids, the Hal Far Fighter Flight making spirited attempts to intercept most of them, these attempts being crowned by success on the 22nd when Flt Lt G. Burges managed to shoot down an SM 79 tri-motor bomber. In Egypt, at the end of the month, 80 Squadron had sufficient Hurricanes to form a complete flight of these, and four could also be spared to return to Malta to aid in the defence.

In the Desert a pattern was developing; SM 79s made attacks on Alexandria and units of the British fleet, defending Gladiators and Blenheim 1Fs finding it difficult to intercept these swift aircraft. Blenheims kept up a series of attacks on Italian bases and communications, and on troop concentrations, the Italian fighters finding it almost as difficult to reach decisive conclusions with these, as did the British fighters with the SM 79s. Over the front fighters and army support aircraft frequently clashed, while at night lumbering SM 81s bombed Alexandria, and Bombays of 216 Squadron retaliated by raiding Tobruk.

After several successful fights late in June, 33 Squadron's Gladiators achieved their best results on July 4th; after a combat in the morning when two CR 42s were shot down, they surprised a number of these fighters in the afternoon just as they were taking off, and shot down nine of them without loss. During July however, 202 Group was weakened by the withdrawal of 45 Squadron, which took its Blenheims to the Sudan to join in the fighting now taking place over East Africa. The overall strength of RAF Middle East was increased, however, by the arrival of the Short Sunderland flying-boats of 228 Squadron from the United Kingdom, these joining 230 Squadron (another recent arrival) on operations from Alexandria and Malta. The crews of these heavily-armed aircraft had on occasion to be reprimanded for their zeal in looking for fights; on July 28th two aircraft of 230 Squadron 'trailed their coats' along the coast of Sicily while on reconnaissance sorties, both attracting the attention of formations of the latest Macchi 200 fighters. One Sunderland was badly damaged, but the gunners of the boat sent a Macchi down into the sea, a second being claimed damaged;

gunners on the second aircraft also claimed to have shot down a Macchi. Along the Libyan coast Italian fighters were frequently in combat with 228 Squadron's aircraft, as these reported on the movements of shipping in and out of the African ports, CR 42s finally shooting down one of the big aircraft near Tobruk on August 5th.

During July Malta continued to suffer occasional raids, the biggest day being the 16th when the defending fighters and anti-aircraft guns made about ten claims for the loss of one fighter. Another of the defenders was lost on the 31st but, by this time, some fourteen victories had been claimed since the commencement of hostilities. The largest reinforcement to date arrived on August 2nd when 12 Hurricanes of 418 Flight flew off the aircraft carrier *Argus*, to land on the island; the surviving aircraft of the Fighter Flight were combined with these to form 261 Squadron, the first new unit to be formed in the Mediterranean since the start of the war.

In Africa, 'B' Flight of 80 Squadron had moved its Gladiators to Sidi Barrani on August 1st to relieve the 33 Squadron flight there, but three days later the unit made an inauspicious start when four of its fighters escorted a 208 Squadron Lysander over the front, becoming engaged with several formations of CR 32s, CR 42s and Ba 65s. Although claims for four of the Italian aircraft were made, three of the Gladiators were shot down; two pilots managed to bale out, both of whom were soon to render outstanding service and make their names as leading fighter pilots; they were Flt Lt M. T. St J. Pattle, later probably the RAF's top-scoring pilot of the war, and Flg Off P. Wyke-ham-Barnes. As a result of this increase in Italian fighter activity, 80 Squadron's second Gladiator-equipped flight joined the first at the front on August 8th, and that same afternoon the combined flights crossed the front on patrol and engaged a large force of CR 42s, claiming nine destroyed and six probables for the loss of two Gladiators, in a whirling dogfight reminiscent of those fought over the Western Front in 1917–18.

A few French aircrews from the various French possessions in the Middle East had by now escaped to continue the fight with the RAF, some of them bringing their aircraft with them, and on August 12th the first Free French Flight was attached to 80 Squadron's Hurricane Flight at Amriya, adding two Morane 406 fighters and two Potez 63–11 reconnaissance-bombers to the operational strength.

Italian seaplanes and flying-boats were appearing more frequently along the Egyptian coast at this time, and on August 15th Blenheim 1Fs of 30 Squadron and Blenheim 1 bombers of 55 Squadron made a low-level attack on their base at Bomba, on the Libyan coast, in an effort to put an end to these flights. On the 17th 80 Squadron Gladiators caught a Cant flying-boat over the sea near the front and shot it down, and on this date also, the elusive SM 79s were at last brought to bay. Over Alexandria some twenty-seven of the bombers in several formations attacked shipping at anchor, but they were met by Gladiators of 112 Squadron, which claimed two shot down; one of 80 Squadron's Hurricanes which had just moved to Mersa Matruh on detachment, joined the fray, and in quick succession Flg Off J. Lapsley shot down three of the bombers.

Another new fighter squadron came into existence on August 19th when 80 Squadron's Hurricane Flight and 'C' Flight of 33 Squadron, together with the Free French Flight, combined to form 274 Squadron, the first all-Hurricane unit in the Middle East. Four days later 3 Squadron of the Royal Australian Air Force arrived in Egypt where it began forming on Gladiators, Gauntlets and Lysanders for army co-operation duties.

On September 1st the Italians began massing along the Egyptian frontier, and at once a flight of 112 Squadron moved to Sidi Barrani to relieve 'B' Flight of 80 Squadron, which then took up station at Sidi Haneish. Detachments of Hurricanes and fighter-Blenheims were also moved forward, and when ten SM 79s raided Sidi Barrani on the 10th, sixteen fighters met them, five bombers being claimed shot down, two by Flg Off Lapsley in a Hurricane. Marshal Graziani's forces moved into Egypt on the 13th with four divisions and 200 tanks, and the British patrol occupying Sollum withdrew in the face of this overwhelming force.

With Sidi Barrani threatened, the rest of the fighters here moved back to Sidi Haneish, and reinforcements were urgently requested, 6 and 84 Squadrons being sent forward to Egypt from Palestine and Iraq. At the same time one flight of 33 Squadron began converting to Hurricanes. The Italians had also brought in air reinforcements and a number of combats took place during the next weeks as their advance moved slowly eastwards. By the 18th they were fifteen miles east of Sidi Barrani, but here they stopped and the advance petered out.

Meanwhile some Vickers Wellington heavy bombers had now reached Egypt, and these replaced the Valentias of 70 Squadron, making their first raid during the night of September 18–19th on the docks at Benghazi, a target previously beyond the range of RAF bombers. Other reinforcements arrived on the 26th when the first four Blenheims and five Hurricanes to reach Egypt since the fall of France, flew in via a new route across the Sahara from Takoradi in West Africa, to where they had been delivered by ship. The vast majority of air reinforcements were to use this route during the next two years.

The Blenheim squadrons were now making progressively heavier attacks on targets at, or near the front, and wing raids by four or five squadrons with fighter escort were now becoming the norm. 45 Squadron had returned from the Sudan now, making six squadrons of these bombers available. Combats over the front remained fairly frequent but generally on a small scale; an exception occurred on October 31st when the new Hurricanes of 33 Squadron engaged SM 79s and their CR escort claiming three bombers and one fighter for the loss of two Hurricanes. Gladiators of 112 Squadron then joined the combat, claiming three more fighters for the loss of four of their own number, although three of these were not lost to enemy action.

On Malta occasional alerts still occurred, but these became less frequent as the autumn wore on. During September three American-built Martin Maryland reconnaissance-bombers, taken over from French contracts, arrived on the island and 431 Flight was formed with these and a lone Blackburn Skua, for general reconnaissance purposes. The Maryland was a fast and well-armed aircraft as was shown on October 30th when Plt Off A. Warburton in one of them shot down an Italian seaplane.

At this juncture a new and unexpected factor arose; Mussolini invaded Greece from Albania. Britain at once offered aid, but the Greek government, afraid of provoking German intervention, declined the offer of British troops, though gladly accepted assistance in the air. This of course, could only be given at the expense of the RAF in Egypt, but none the less, the decision was made, and on November 1st 30 Squadron flew its fighter-Blenheims to Eleusis for the defence of Athens, at the same time converting some of its aircraft back to bomber configuration for offensive purposes.

A detachment of six Wellingtons from 70 Squadron followed the Blenheims to Eleusis on the 6th and on this date 30 Squadron's bomber flight raided the Valona area; defending fighters intercepted and most of the Blenheims were damaged. The next day the six Wellingtons repeated the raid, but again fighters were up and two bombers were shot down, two more being damaged. After this, all further raids by Wellingtons were made under cover of darkness. 84 Squadron arrived on the 8th, and on the 14th sent three Blenheims over the front; two were lost to enemy action and a third damaged. As though to reinforce this proof that the bombers should not operate alone, three 30 Squadron aircraft over the same area next day also lost one of their number. 80 Squadron was then ordered to the new battle zone, 'B' Flight arriving on the 18th, and at once engaging in combat on the 19th when in a big battle over the front line nine CR 42s were claimed shot down. A few days later 211 Squadron joined the expeditionary air force, and on the 28th 80 Squadron was again in combat over the front, claiming seven fighters and two probables for the loss of one Gladiator.

To offset this drain on Egypt, two new Wellington squadrons were flown in during the month from Bomber Command in England, 38 Squadron going straight to Shallufa, where it was joined in December by 37 Squadron after this latter unit's aircraft had first undertaken several missions from Malta. Two flights of 3 RAAF Squadron also moved up ready for operations with Gladiators and Gauntlets, and on November 19th four of the former on reconnaissance were attacked by eighteen CR 42s, which shot down one Gladiator for the loss of at least three of their number. On the 20th 112 Squadron's Gladiators spotted many Italian fighters attacking a Lysander and a Blenheim, and their Hurricane escort over Sidi Barrani, and waded in, claiming eight for no loss. 274 Squadron moved up to the front on the 23rd and four days later a veteran Hurricane unit from England, 73 Squadron, flew off the carrier *Furious* to Takoradi. The pilots at once began to negotiate the tortuous route across Africa to Egypt, but unfortunately the first six Hurricanes to set out ran out of fuel and all crash-landed.

Malta too received some reinforcement when another twelve Hurricanes flew off *Argus* on November 17th, but on this occasion the range had been miscalculated, only four reaching the island, the others having to ditch in the sea when their fuel ran out. Late in the month there was a small awakening of activity and in two days 261 Squadron claimed three victories, but generally all was reasonably quiet.

Despite the loss of units to Greece and the much greater numbers of opposing Italian forces, General Wavell, the British Supreme Commander in the Middle East, now planned a daring reconnaissance in strength, ordering his forces to be prepared to follow up any opportunities this offered. Early in December his troops began moving up ready for this venture, and, to support this, 202 Group mustered thirteen squadrons, with a fourteenth to join them at the earliest possible date. These units were: 33 and 274 Squadrons, both now fully equipped with Hurricane 1s; 3 RAAF Squadron with Gladiators and Gauntlets; 6 Squadron with Lysanders; 208 Squadron with one flight of its Lysanders recently replaced by Hurricanes for low-level, high speed reconnaissance over enemy territory; 55 Squadron, in the process of replacing its

Blenheim 1s with Mark 4s; 45 Squadron with Blenheim 1s; 11 and 39 Squadrons with Blenheim 1s, which had been sent north from Aden specially for this operation; 37, 38 and 70 Squadrons with Wellingtons, and 216 Squadron with Bombays, all in the Nile Delta, and available for night bombing operations; The fourteenth unit was, of course, 73 Squadron.

Early on the 9th the offensive opened with an attack on camps at Nibeiwa; close air cover was provided from the start, and all fighters were ordered to strafe if they had any ammunition left during their return from patrols. The advance was an immediate success, and led at once to a great increase in aerial activity. 274 Squadron was much to the fore on the first day, claiming eight fighters and four SM 79s. On the 10th Sidi Barrani was retaken and the Italians were in obvious trouble; Wavell now took a gamble, ordering the 4th Indian Division to East Africa and bringing in the inexperienced 6th Australian Division to continue the advance.

After a number of dive-bomber sorties during the initial three days, the Gauntlets of 3 RAAF Squadron were now withdrawn, but the next day the unit's Gladiators were badly 'bounced' by CR 42s, five being shot down while only two of the attackers could be claimed. On the 14th the first pilots and aircraft of 73 Squadron were ready for action, and moved forward initially on attachment to 274 Squadron; by the 15th all Italian forces had been cleared out of Egypt. Air activity then fell to a reduced scale until Italian reinforcements could arrive, but by the 23rd 33 Squadron alone had claimed thirty-six destroyed and ten probables since the offensive began.

The Australians opened the assault on Bardia on January 3rd, 1941, supported by naval bombardment, and this brought the Regia Aeronautica out in force again. Sgt A. E. Marshall of 73 Squadron caught five SM 79s bombing HMS *Terror* near the port, and rapidly shot down three, damaging a fourth. During the next few days there was considerable combat in the air, mainly over the Gambut area, and here the first Italian monoplane fighters, Fiat G-50s, were met. By the 9th Flg Off E. M. Mason of 274 Squadron, in a series of raids on Italian airfields, had brought his personal score to thirteen – the highest at that time achieved in the Mediterranean area.

As the month drew on, Italian air reaction again declined, and further squadrons could be released. 11 Squadron took its Blenheims to Greece, and 39 Squadron withdrew to re-equip with Marylands. On the ground the advance continued, Tobruk being attacked on the 21st and quickly falling, Derna then being taken on the 30th.

Elsewhere at this time all was not well. Over Malta during December Sgt F. N. Robertson of 261 Squadron had shot down a bomber at night on the 18th – probably the first night victory in the Mediterranean, and on Christmas Eve Flg Off Warburton of 431 Flight claimed an SM 79 near Naples while on a reconnaissance in this area. By the close of 1940 the fighters had claimed forty-five Italian aircraft destroyed, probably destroyed or damaged, and to these were added four shot down on January 9th, 1941. The next day the blow fell.

Worried by his ally's rapid collapse in Africa, Adolf Hitler decided to send limited German forces to the area in an effort to bolster the defence and save the situation; at this stage he had no intention of allowing himself to become embroiled in a long drawn-out campaign. First German units to arrive were elements of the Luftwaffe which landed in Sicily early in January, and on the 10th, Ju 87 dive-bombers launched a violent and brilliantly-executed attack on the aircraft carrier *Illustrious*, severely damaging her. The carrier's Fulmar fighters put up the best defence they could, then flying to Malta, where 261 Squadron was also in the air, claiming four or five more victories during the day. *Illustrious* limped into Grand Harbour at Valetta, and the Germans then began a determined attempt to finish her off.

The first big raid came on the 16th, four Hurricanes and three Fulmars taking the air and claiming five raiders, while the guns claimed five more. Further heavy raids followed on the 18th and the 19th, every available fighter taking off to intercept, and by the end of this four day assault, forty enemy aircraft had been claimed, twenty-three by fighters and seventeen by guns; during the fighting on the 19th Flt Lt J. A. F. Maclachlan claimed four confirmed destroyed and one probable. After the 20th the assault tailed-off, and on the 23rd *Illustrious* was sufficiently repaired to allow her to leave the island and limp to safety – and many months of repair in an American shipyard.

In Greece early in December a detachment of Gladiators of 112 Squadron had arrived, and operations had continued as in the previous month, Blenheims of 30, 84, 211, and newly-arrived 113 Squadrons making raids over Valona and on front-line targets, while Gladiators of 80 Squadron flew patrols over the front. Bombers had been intercepted on the 19th when 14 Gladiators, which were on detachment at Yanina, met five SM 79s and shot down one for one loss. The next day three bombers were claimed, and on the 21st in a big dogfight, eight CR 42s were shot down for the loss of two Gladiators, though one of these was flown by the commanding officer, Sqn Ldr Hickey. On the 22nd Blenheims of 84 Squadron raided Albania, but were attacked by

Macchi 200s, which shot down two of the bombers and damaged five more.

80 Squadron was then relieved by a squadron of Greek Gladiators and withdrew to the Athens area; by this time the weather was seriously reducing activity in the air, though on December 30th 30 Squadron's fighter Blenheims gained their first success in Greece, shooting down two Z.506B floatplanes. On January 18th, 1941, the main part of 112 Squadron arrived in Greece, followed by 11 Squadron, and late in the month 80 Squadron intercepted some sporadic raids on Athens, shooting down one or two bombers.

The Luftwaffe Arrives
in Africa

With the departure of *Illustrious* from Malta, some of the Luftwaffe units left Sicily and moved on late in January to Tripoli, in Libya, where German army units were due soon to disembark. By early February, however, the Italians were in general retreat from the Libyan province of Cyrenaica, and on the 4th the 7th Armoured Division of the British Army began an arduous journey across a desert track from Mechili, by-passing the whole of the Cyrenaican 'bulge' and the coastal road along which the Italians were moving. This gamble paid off, as the British column was able to overtake virtually the whole Italian Army and cut the road west of Benghazi. On February 6th the Italians threw themselves in desperation at the British forces blocking their retreat, in the Battle of Beda Fomm. When this ended the Italian 10th Army had been totally defeated, 130,000 prisoners being taken together with 1,300 guns, and 400 tanks to add to the already enormous tally gained earlier in the advance. The victorious forces then moved up to positions in front of the El Agheila line, and here they halted, exhausted. The whole two month campaign had cost them just 500 dead, 1,373 wounded and 55 missing. On February 8th Marshal Graziani resigned.

At this point the RAF was further weakened; 33 Squadron had already pulled back into Egypt ready to go to Greece, and 274 Squadron now handed its Hurricanes to 3 RAAF Squadron, which became a full fighter unit, and withdrew to Egypt to rest. This left the whole fighter defence of Cyrenaica in the hands of the Australian unit at Benina, and 73 Squadron at Tobruk – and the Germans were pouring into Tripoli fast now.

Luftwaffe aircraft had been appearing over the front in small numbers for some days when 3 RAAF Squadron made its first claim against the Germans on February 15th, shooting down a reconnaissance Ju 88. Two days later elements of both fighter squadrons engaged Ju 87s bombing positions at Marsa Brega and claimed eight shot down; on the 19th 3 RAAF again intercepted Ju 87s, this time escorted by Bf 110s, and the first two Hurricanes were lost to the Germans. The 7th Armoured Division now withdrew into Egypt to re-form, only skeleton forces being left at the front. On the 20th two new Italian divisions arrived in Tripoli to join the German units there; as though courting disaster, a substantial proportion of the fresher army units available to the British command, were now sent to Greece, the government of which had finally agreed to a full expeditionary force being sent, and to serve them, 208 Squadron left with its Hurricanes and Lysanders, one flight of 6 Squadron then being re-equipped with Hurricanes to carry on the tactical reconnaissance duties in the Desert.

Throughout March there was a lull, with little activity on either side, and the opportunity was taken to withdraw 45 Squadron for re-equipment with Blenheim 4s, 55 Squadron remaining as the only day-bomber squadron available for immediate action.

Over Malta a reduced force of German and Italian aircraft from Sicily kept 261 Squadron on its toes, newly arrived Messerschmitt Bf 109Es proving a particular embarrassment to the Hurricanes. These fighters shot down three Hurricanes on February 4th and another on the 12th, while on the 16th Flt Lt Maclachlan was shot down and lost an arm. During these weeks four Ju 88s and a CR 42 were brought down, but none of the Messerschmitts could be destroyed. Late in the month new Luftwaffe units moved into Sicily, and a renewed assault began. On the 26th came a big raid, eight Hurricanes getting off to claim two confirmed and eleven probables, while the guns claimed five, but five Hurricanes were shot down. On the ground Luqa was put out of action, six Wellingtons which had recently arrived from England being destroyed and seven badly damaged. By the end of the month the fighters' total tally had risen to ninety-six, but their own losses had been sixteen aircraft and eleven pilots during the one month.

In early March more heavy raids were made, but in these the results were more favourable, fourteen raiders being claimed for the loss of two Hurricanes, while the guns claimed ten more. Bf 109s then carried out a series of attacks on 228 Squadron's Sunderlands, riding at anchor in Kalafrana Bay, sinking one and damaging two others. Following these attacks the last Wellingtons and Sunderlands left for Egypt. The raids then eased off as more Axis units moved to Africa,

until March 23rd when a supply convoy approached the island, five
raids then being thrown in. By this time 261 Squadron had been
strengthened by the arrival of a flight of 274 Squadron from Egypt, led
by Flt Lt E. M. Mason, and fourteen Hurricanes were able to rise to
the defence, claiming nine attackers for no loss, the guns claiming four
more. On April 3rd twelve Hurricane 2As were flown off the carrier
Ark Royal to the island to replenish the defences, but the Germans now
had bigger things afoot, and were leaving Sicily by this time for bases
further north.

February was a good month for the RAF in Greece, the weather
allowing an increase in activity. On the 13th the first attempts were
made to escort Blenheims on their raids by Gladiators, but the fighters
lost their charges in clouds, and the bombers were again intercepted,
three being lost. On the 17th, however, the first six Hurricanes arrived,
going to 80 Squadron at a forward base at Paramytha. Two days later
seventeen Hurricanes of 33 Squadron arrived at Eleusis, and on the
20th 80 Squadron Hurricanes escorted eighteen Blenheims over the
front and shot down four attacking Fiat G-50s. Gladiators were in the
area escorting supply-dropping aircraft, and these saw other fighters
following the British formation back, and at once attacked these,
claiming another four.

On the 23rd 11 Squadron began operations, and a flight of 33 Squadron joined 80 at Paramythia. On the 27th nine Hurricanes escorted a
similar number of Blenheims to Valona and claimed nine intercepting
fighters, while during the next day a series of heavy combats occurred
over the whole front, fighters of 80 and 112 Squadrons claiming twenty-
six and nine probables, Plt Off R. N. Cullen claiming five and Flt Lt
Pattle four and a probable; the Italians subsequently denied that their
losses were anything like this level.

More combats followed, and on March 3rd two 80 Squadron Hurricanes intercepted five Cant Z1007 bombers, claiming all shot down,
four by Cullen. The next day, however, Cullen failed to return from
an escort mission, having been credited with sixteen and a half victories
in a very short space of time. By this time too, Pattle's score had risen
to twenty-one, making him the RAF top-scorer in the Mediterranean
up to this date.

Now 80 Squadron flew back to Eleusis to rest, duties over the front
being maintained by 112 Squadron and a detachment of 33. 37 Squadron, which had been maintaining a detachment of Wellingtons in
Greece since early February, now moved over altogether. During mid-
March 33 and 112 Squadrons during patrols over the front, frequently

met large enemy formations, and between the 9th and the 14th these two units claimed at least thirty-two victories for minimal loss.

Late in the month Pattle was posted from 80 Squadron to command 33, and at the same time reinforcements of Hurricanes and Blenheims arrived from Egypt to bring squadrons up to strength to support the expeditionary force which was now arriving, in its activities. At this moment fate was about to deal Britain and her few allies a savage blow, and in a few days the victories in Africa and in the skies over Greece were to be turned to ashes.

On March 31st General Erwin Rommel, the new German commander in Africa, began a reconnaissance in strength to probe the British defences, and quickly pushed to Marsa Brega. In the face of this, the dreadfully weakened defenders withdrew to Agedabia, and Rommel, seizing the initiative, at once pushed ahead. Within hours the British were in headlong retreat back into Egypt, but worse was still to come. Determined to clear his right flank before his projected invasion of Russia, Hitler now ordered his forces into Yugoslavia and Greece, and on April 6th a full scale invasion of both countries began, backed by strong elements of the Luftwaffe.

The RAF immediately retaliated, Blenheims bombing German convoys in Yugoslavia from April 7th, while on that date Sqn Ldr Pattle led 33 Squadron on a sweep up the Rupel Pass in Bulgaria, five Bf 109s being claimed shot down here. Although initial sorties were successful, Axis air strength was so overwhelming that the picture soon became dark indeed, and by the 11th German aircraft had begun a series of heavy assaults on Allied airfields. Very swiftly the position of a flight of Sunderlands of 230 Squadron which had been operating from the Greek coast, became untenable, and they withdrew to Suda Bay, Crete, while the Wellingtons also withdrew, then undertaking a sustained night offensive against the invaders from their base in the Delta.

On April 13th Blenheim squadrons carried out a number of successful raids, but during the day a complete formation of six bombers from 211 Squadron failed to return, only two crewmen surviving. 33 Squadron was now taking a fair toll of the raiders, enjoying a particularly successful day on the 14th when nine were claimed, five of them by Pattle, whose personal score was climbing very rapidly. Next day Bf 109s, Ju 88s and G-50s swept over Larissa plain all day, catching 113 Squadron on the ground and damaging or destroying all its Blenheims. 80 Squadron claimed five Ju 88s, but a section of Hurricanes of 33 Squadron were 'bounced' by Bf 109s while taking off, and two were shot down; one Messerschmitt was hit by the survivor and crash-landed on the airfield.

The Allied armies were in full retreat through Greece now, and on the 16th the Blenheim units all withdrew to the Athens area, while 208 Squadron lost two of its Lysanders to German fighters. On the 18th 30 Squadron, its Blenheim fighters outclassed by the opposition, withdrew to Crete to undertake convoy patrols from here. The Hurricanes engaged in several further fierce combats during this period, the climax coming on the 20th when nine 80 Squadron aircraft and six from 33 Squadron engaged 90 Axis aircraft over Athens, claiming fifteen shot down. The cost was high, however, as both Sqn Ldr Pattle, by now as it later transpired, probably the top-scoring RAF pilot of World War II, and Flt Lt Woods, DFC, veteran of Malta's early defence, were shot down and killed, three other Hurricanes also being lost, though two of the pilots managed to bale out.

More Blenheims had been destroyed on the ground during this week of incessant raids, and all remaining bomber squadrons now began withdrawing to Crete. On April 22nd the remaining eighteen Hurricanes of 33, 80 and 208 Squadrons moved to Argos where, on the next day, five reinforcement aircraft arrived. Just as these landed a large formation of Bf 110s attacked without warning, and although four of the new arrivals managed to get back into the air, thirteen Hurricanes were destroyed on the ground. The pilots who got airborne were able to gain several more victories, four being credited to Sgt G. E. C. Reynolds of 33 Squadron alone. It was the end in Greece, and over the next few days the surviving Hurricanes withdrew to Crete. From this island the few remaining bombers of 11, 84 and 211 Squadrons together with the last flyable Greek aircraft, left for Egypt. At the same time five Blenheim 4Fs of 203 Squadron, newly-arrived from Aden, moved to Crete for convoy protection duties.

In the Desert, meanwhile, the retreat was in full spate, and Luftwaffe aircraft were appearing more frequently. On April 3rd Hurricanes of 3 RAAF Squadron met Ju 87s and Bf 110s, three bombers and five fighters being claimed, four of the fighters by Flg Off P. Turnbull. Two days later both this unit and 73 Squadron met formations of Ju 87s on two separate occasions, fourteen being claimed in all for a loss of two Hurricanes.

The whole army in Africa suffered a severe loss on the 6th when General O'Connor, the brilliant field commander who had led the rapid advance of the past months, was captured near Derna. By now British forces had withdrawn to this area, and the port of Tobruk was being reinforced, all other forces then being ordered to defensive positions on the Egyptian frontier at Mersa Matruh; on the 8th, however, the 2nd Armoured Division was cut off at Derna and largely overrun. The next day 73 Squadron began flying operations from within the Tobruk perimeter, and on the 10th Axis forces reached this perimeter, the port then entering a state of siege.

The first big air attack on Tobruk came on the 14th, by which time 73 Squadron had been reinforced by the Free French Fighter Flight from Egypt, and a series of violent combats commenced. The climax came on the 23rd when three Hurricanes were shot down and one destroyed on the ground, while another from 6 Squadron's Hurricane Flight which was also based in the fortress, also failed to return; six enemy aircraft were claimed shot down. By this time 73 Squadron had almost ceased to exist as a fighting unit, and on the 25th the survivors withdrew to Egypt, leaving only the 6 Squadron contingent to soldier on.

The first Messerschmitt Bf 109 fighters had appeared over the front at this time, being met initially on April 19th by 274 Squadron, which had returned to action, and in this engagement two Hurricanes were shot down, one being flown by the commanding officer, Sqn Ldr J. Lapsley, DFC, who was badly wounded; it was a black portent of what was to come.

By this time the East African campaign was virtually over, and the majority of the units there could be spared for the Libyan desert. The South African government now agreed that units of the SAAF might operate this far north of the Union, and one of the first squadrons to arrive in Egypt from Abyssinia was 1 SAAF Squadron, flying Hurricanes; in consequence of this timely reinforcement, 3 RAAF Squadron was withdrawn to re-equip with American-built Curtiss Tomahawk fighters, which were just arriving in the Middle East.

During the last days of the month 73 and 274 Squadrons undertook a number of ground attacks on Axis forces, but at the same time the Hurricanes began to suffer regular losses to the new Bf 109s. 39 Squadron returned to the front with its new Marylands in a general reconnaissance role, but this unit also quickly lost two aircraft to the potent new foe. On May 8th the last Hurricane of 6 Squadron evacuated Tobruk, and in the Desert all RAF units were now back in Egypt.

On Crete late in April the tattered remnants of the units from Greece were preparing to meet the expected onslaught; many of the longer-serving fighter pilots were sent back to Egypt, and fresh reinforcements sent out, together with some Royal Navy fighters and pilots of 805 Squadron. Initially the Hurricanes achieved some successes against the first probing attacks of the Luftwaffe, and the score of Flg Off W. Vale of 80 Squadron in particular rose swiftly. Early in May the Blenheim fighters of 30 and 203 Squadrons left the island, leaving the handful of Hurricanes and Gladiators to hold the fort.

Air attacks began in earnest on May 12th, and on the 14th very heavy fighter assaults were made on the British airfields. Unserviceability and damage due to strafing attacks cut the number of defending aircraft available, but the pilots fought desperately with what they had, and a substantial number of raiders were shot down by the 18th when operations ceased, and the survivors made their way by various routes to Egypt. The Germans now launched a massive airborne invasion of the island, and the only resistance which could be offered in the air was by aircraft which had made the long flight from Egypt.

Just as the air assault had begun on Crete, a convoy had docked in Alexandria bringing fifty new Hurricanes and a substantial number of tanks, and these were at once issued to units in order that a counter-attack in the Desert might be launched forthwith under the code-name 'Operation Brevity'. It was indeed brief, the British forces being thrown back with heavy losses on the first day!

Attention was then turned on Crete, and on the 20th Marylands of 39 Squadron flew patrols over the island, shooting down a number of Junkers 52 transports. Two days later Blenheims and Wellingtons bombed German positions on the island, and long-range Hurricanes of 73 Squadron began patrols. 14 Squadron had arrived from East Africa with its Blenheims, and opened operations with an attack on Axis positions on the Egyptian frontier, but the unescorted bombers were intercepted by Bf 109s and five were lost. At this point there was a further small, but welcome influx of Hurricanes. Aircraft of 213 and 229 Squadrons from England had flown off the aircraft carrier *Furious* to Malta, and from there flew on to Egypt. For initial operations the pilots of the latter unit were attached to 274 Squadron and of the former to 73. Another bomber squadron, 24 SAAF, also arrived from East Africa, newly re-equipped with Marylands.

For the rest of the month operations were divided between patrols over convoys supplying Tobruk, and long-range missions to Crete. On May 25th Blenheims of 14 Squadron destroyed at least a dozen Ju 52s on the ground at Maleme; they returned for a second attack, but lost three aircraft on this occasion. Hurricanes of 274 Squadron were also over the island, losing three of their number, and the next day four more Blenheims were lost here, two of 14 Squadron and two of 55. Marylands of 24 SAAF Squadron, co-operating with Hurricanes, then achieved a number of successes, but the last mission over the island was completed on the 31st. The next day the first Beaufighters of 272

Squadron arrived in Egypt from England, where they had undertaken a few missions, and immediately they went out to escort in the last of the shipping as the evacuation of Crete came to an end.

Not only in Crete and Egypt had the Axis struck; more subtly their influence had produced problems to the rear, in Iraq. Pro-Axis elements under Rashid Ali had gained power and now, encouraged by British reversals elsewhere, began to threaten Allied security here. Matters came to a head late in April with the landing of additional British troops from India against Iraqi wishes. At once their troops moved to surround the large RAF base at Habbaniyah where 4 Flying Training School was situated, and strenuous attempts were made by the British to provide a viable air component here, as on the ground the Iraqis were in vastly superior numbers. At Aqir in Palestine were the Blenheims of 84 Squadron, and a new squadron, 250, which was forming on Tomahawks. At Habbaniyah the Audax and Oxford trainers were fitted with bomb racks and prepared for operations as the Air Striking Force, while a few Gladiators used for fighter training, formed the Fighter Flight. Crews were to be provided by the instructors and the more promising pupils. In South Iraq was one further squadron, 244, still with its Vincents, and the aircraft carrier *Hermes* with a number of Fairey Swordfish aircraft aboard, was patrolling just off the coast.

At once detachments of Wellingtons from 37 and 70 Squadrons, and Blenheim 4Fs of 203 Squadron, just back from Crete, were rushed from Egypt, and at dawn on May 2nd Wellingtons and aircraft from Habbaniyah attacked the Iraqi forces investing the base, keeping up the assault throughout the day. Aircraft from the four and a half squadrons of the Iraqi Air Force attempted retaliatory attacks, but with little effect. In the south British troops at Basra took over the airfield and other key positions, attacking Iraqi troops in the area, supported by Vincents and Swordfish.

On May 3rd the Wellingtons turned their attack on the Iraqi airfields, leaving the fighting around Habbaniyah to the Air Striking Force trainers; the bombers were assisted in their new task by the Blenheim fighters of 203 Squadron which began moving into Habbaniyah itself on this date. At the same time Valentias and Douglas DC-2s of 31 Squadron, which had flown to southern Iraq from India, began flying troops into the beleaguered camp and flying out non-combatant personnel and families. A relief force, to be known as 'Habforce', was marshalled at Pumping Station H4 on the Transjordan border to move to the relief of the garrison, and a small detachment of six Blenheims from 84 and 203 Squadrons was attached to this force to provide air support.

Long before this force arrived however, the Iraqis were seen on May 6th to be leaving their positions around Habbaniyah, and the Air Striking Force aircraft kept up a sustained attack, transforming the withdrawal into a near rout, while the regular squadrons maintained the attack on the Iraqi airfields. Two days later a detachment of pilots from 94 Squadron arrived from Egypt with some Gladiators, and joined the garrison, although on the 12th the Wellingtons returned to Egypt, the main threat now being over. At this stage, in answer to Iraqi appeals for help, a contingent of German aircraft began to arrive, staging through landing grounds in Syria. A Blenheim of 203 Squadron spotted some of these on the ground at the Syrian airfield of Palmyra, and an attack was at once made by Blenheims of 84 and 203 Squadrons, and two Tomahawks of 250 Squadron – the very first action for these new fighters. Another Blenheim squadron, 211, just back from Crete, now arrived at Aqir and began flights over Syria looking for other German aircraft.

The first German raid came on May 16th, when three He 111s attacked Habbaniyah, doing more damage in the one attack than the Iraqis had managed to inflict throughout their assault. The bombers were intercepted by a Gladiator of 94 Squadron, and one was shot down, but the fighter was itself brought down by the concentrated defensive fire of the other two. The next day two Gladiators flew to Rashid airfield where they caught two Bf 110s just taking off, and shot down both.

'Habforce' arrived at Habbaniyah on the 18th, and joined by units from the garrison it moved at once on the Iraqi troops who had set up positions at Fallujah; the British forces were supported by the Air Striking Force, which had been reinforced with some crews from 208 Squadron. German activities in the air were increasing, and reached a climax on the 25th with a number of indecisive combats, but repeated RAF attacks on the airfields rapidly reduced the effectiveness of the Luftwaffe component to a low level. On the 29th the first Italian CR 42s were met, and one was shot down by a Gladiator after it had forced down an Audax; by the next day, however, 'Habforce' had reached the walls of Baghdad, whereupon Rashid Ali and his supporters fled and the city officials requested a truce to discuss terms. An armistice was signed on the 31st, all remaining German and Italian aircraft and personnel quickly leaving the country. With hostilities over, the Air Striking Force became again 4 FTS, while 203 Squadron and the personnel of 94 Squadron returned to Egypt, 211 Squadron handing its Blenheims to 11 Squadron, which had just arrived in Palestine without aircraft; 211 then left for the Sudan where it was to operate for several months as an Operational Training Unit.

During this period the situation on Malta had changed radically; throughout the second half of April the German Messerschmitts appeared on occasions, on the 13th shooting down and wounding Flt Lt E. M. Mason, DFC, after he had despatched one of their number. Twenty-three reinforcement Hurricanes flew in from *Ark Royal* on the 27th, and the airfield at Takali was then given over to the fighters. Late in the month there was a flurry of activity when six Hurricanes were lost between April 28th and May 1st for a claim of nine Axis aircraft shot down and six probables; during a big battle with Bf 109s on May 6th four more Hurricanes failed to return, but on the 8th a further batch of reinforcements flew in, joined by 16 Beaufighters of 252 Squadron, newly-arrived from the United Kingdom.

On May 12th 185 Squadron was formed at Hal Far, there now being some fifty Hurricane 2As and Bs on the island, and the next day the new squadron was blooded, losing one aircraft to a Bf 109. Shortly after this, however, the last of the German aircraft left Sicily for the impending invasion of Russia, and with the removal of their ever-present threat, Malta was then rapidly reinforced. During April a flotilla of destroyers had begun operations from the island, and now Blenheims of Bomber Command's 2 Group were to be dispatched on attachment to provide an effective anti-shipping strike force. The first of these, six aircraft of 82 Squadron, arrived on May 17th, and on the 21st came another mass arrival of Hurricanes, this time from *Furious*. This latest batch was not composed of the usual replacements, but comprised the aircraft and pilots of three squadrons, 213, 229 and 249. The two former units flew on after refuelling, led by the Beaufighters of 252 Squadron, which now moved on to Egypt, and they were joined by 261 Squadron which exchanged its own tired aircraft for the newer ones of 249 Squadron, then moving to the Middle East for a well-earned rest. Early in June another sixteen Hurricanes, this time from 46 Squadron, also arrived, it being intended that these too should fly on to Egypt, but in the event they were retained on the island. It should be pointed out that at this stage neither 46 or 249 Squadrons were accompanied by any ground crew personnel, relying on the Malta garrison for all non-flying aid.

Taking advantage of the absence of the Luftwaffe in Sicily, another big consignment of forty-eight Hurricanes was flown from *Ark Royal* and *Victorious* on the 14th, but this time tragedy struck; the fighters flew too far to the south, passing the island without sighting it. Only eleven finally managed to make it to Malta after realizing their error, the others all being forced to ditch in the sea when their fuel ran out.

With the increased striking power now available, a concerted attack was launched on Axis shipping passing between Europe and North Africa, and a growing toll was taken. The Italians mounted a number of raids on the island in an effort to neutralize this damaging offensive, but they were met by the greatly reinforced fighter defences, now including cannon-armed Hurricane 2Cs, and suffered substantial losses. 69 Squadron (which 431 Flight had become early in the year) now also received one or two Hurricanes to supplement its Marylands on recon-naissance duties. Further Blenheims from 110 Squadron arrived late in the month, and at this time the aircraft and pilots of 46 Squadron formed the nucleus of a new unit, 126 Squadron. Other Hurricanes, with pilots drawn from all three fighter squadrons, formed the Malta Night Fighter Unit for the defence of the island during the hours of darkness.

In Egypt at the end of May the RAF was fast recovering from its recent depredations, and at this time 45 and 55 Squadrons were both with-drawn to re-equip with new Blenheim 4s, while 30 and 33 Squadrons, now back from Crete, began working up anew, both on Hurricanes. Beaufighters also appeared in the area, the recent arrival of aircraft of 272 Squadron direct from England being followed by 252 Squadron from Malta. At the same time the Hurricanes of 73, 274 and 1 SAAF Squadrons were all fully committed to operations over the front, and for the defence of Alexandria 250 Squadron arrived from Palestine with its new Tomahawks, Flg Off Hamlyn claiming the first success when he shot down a Cant Z. 1007 bomber over the port on June 8th. From East Africa came another SAAF fighter unit, 2 SAAF Squadron, which initially received some Hurricanes. 113 Squadron, also now back in Egypt, was now flying some 'strafer' Blenheim 4s fitted with 20mm cannons, and 238 Hurricane squadron began arriving from the United Kingdom around this time also.

By mid-June General Auchinleck, the new British commander in the Middle East, felt strong enough to launch a new offensive, to be known as 'Operation Battleaxe', and to support this the RAF had available for action over the front, the following units: 1 and 2 SAAF Squadrons – Hurricane 2s; 73 and 274 Squadrons – Hurricane 2s; 250 Squadron –

Tomahawks; 6 Squadron – Lysanders and Hurricanes; 14, 45, 55 and 113 Squadrons – Blenheim 4s; 39 and 24 SAAF Squadrons – Marylands.

'Battleaxe' began on June 14th, making some initial gains, but from the start it was to prove a costly undertaking for the air force as well as for the army. On the first day Hurricanes of 73 Squadron undertook an early morning strafing mission, encountering heavy flak which claimed three pilots, including Flg Off G. Goodman, DFC, a fourteen victory 'ace'. Later in the morning a South African Maryland and an escorting Hurricane were shot down by Bf 109s, the Hurricane being flown by another experienced pilot who could ill be spared, Capt K. Driver, DFC, of 1 SAAF Squadron, who was credited with eleven victories at this time. A second Maryland, this time from 39 Squadron, was also lost, and when other 1 SAAF Squadron Hurricanes attacked some Ju 87s, they lost two of their number to escorting Messerschmitts.

The second day proved even worse; eight Hurricanes were shot down and three damaged against claims for four Bf 109s, and on the 16th another three Hurricanes were lost, although a number of Axis aircraft were shot down. This latter date, which saw the debut of the Tomahawk over the front, also saw the end of the British advance, when an Axis counter-attack, strongly supported by anti-tank guns, brought it to an immediate halt. With the larger part of the British armour destroyed in this encounter, the Allied forces were bludgeoned into withdrawal on the 17th, when at least ten more Hurricanes were lost for ten of the enemy. On the 18th the marauding Bf 109s got amongst the Toma-hawks for the first time, 250 Squadron losing three of its aircraft to these fighters and a fourth to flak. At this stage a composite squadron composed of pilots from 33 Squadron and 806 Squadron, Royal Navy, were thrown into the battle flying Hurricanes, but already all was lost, and by the evening of this day 'Battleaxe' was over. A lull then descended on the desert which was to last many weeks.

While the build-up for 'Battleaxe' had been going on, other British and Commonwealth units had been taking steps to secure the rest of the Middle East. The hostile behaviour of the Vichy authorities in Syria during the troubles in Iraq had led to a decision, pressed by the Free French, to invade and neutralize this French colony. Early in June a force had been gathered on the border between Palestine and Syria, the air component of which comprised the Tomahawks of 3 RAAF Squad-ron, a few Hurricanes of 80 Squadron, 208 Squadron with two flights of Hurricanes and one of Lysanders, 11 Squadron with Blenheim 4s, and 'X' Flight, which had been formed with some of the Gladiators and pilots remaining at Habbaniyah after the siege of that base was lifted.

On June 8th Allied forces moved into Syria, initially in the face of only light resistance, and moved up the coastal road towards Damascus, covered by a Royal Navy cruiser squadron. Fearing just such action the French had flown in substantial reinforcements for their air force, including numbers of the potent Dewoitine 520 fighters, and more units were to arrive throughout June. On the first morning Australian Tomahawks caught six of the newly arrived D-520s on the ground at Rayak and damaged two, but the French fighters quickly showed their metal, shooting down two RN Fulmars over the cruiser squadron and also a reconnaissance Hurricane of 208 Squadron. The next day three Hurricanes joined the Fulmars over the ships, engaging attacking bombers and shooting down at least one, but they were 'bounced' by escorting D-520s which shot down two of the Hurricanes, but then lost at least one of their number to reinforcements of Hurricanes which arrived at the critical moment; they also shot down another Fulmar and damaged two more.

On the ground the advance began to meet increasing resistance, and the RAF was called upon to provide added support here also. The Australian Tomahawks gained their first aerial victories on June 12th when they intercepted a formation of Ju 88s with Italian markings, attempting to bomb the cruisers, and shot down three of them. Over the front the D-520s met their match rather surprisingly on the 15th when they came off worst in a dogfight with 'X' Flight Gladiators; as if to prove that this was no fluke, the biplanes defeated the French fighters even more decisively on the 18th, destroying two for no loss.

With the failure of 'Operation Battleaxe' in the Western Desert, more air units could be released, and 45 Squadron moved its Blenheims to Aquir on the 21st. Pilots of 260 Squadron who had just arrived from England, also moved to this front, being attached initially to 80 Squadron. At the same time 'Habforce', the victors of the brief campaign in Iraq, moved into Syria from this country, and began the long cross-country trek towards the town and airfield of Palmyra. At once the French turned almost the whole of their available air force to attack the column which was without air support, and it was quickly brought to a virtual halt.

Little could be done to provide regular fighter cover to the unfortunate 'Habforce', due to the pressures already on the small air component elsewhere in Syria, but in an effort to ease the situation, a series of fighter strafes on the main French airfields was organized. These attacks were to prove outstandingly successful, and were to swiftly cripple the French air effort. The lessons learnt from this were later to be applied with considerable effect against Axis airfields in Libya.

At last on the 25th some direct cover was provided, and Tomahawks of 3 RAAF Squadron engaged LeO 451 bombers attacking the column, shooting down at least three. The Australians were even more successful when they were able to repeat the patrol on the 28th, every one of six French Naval Martin 167F bombers being shot down in the same area in full view of the greatly-heartened 'Habforce'.

Early in July 84 Squadron again began bombing raids over Syria, and a new squadron, 127, formed from suitable personnel at Habbaniyah, and with the rest of the Hurricanes and Gladiators not already in use by 'X' Flight, moved to an advanced landing ground to cover a further force composed of Indian troops which moved into Northern Syria up the River Euphrates, and pushed towards Deir ez Zor and Aleppo, near the Turkish border. Deir ez Zor fell quickly, and Palmyra was also at last taken by 'Habforce', all surviving French aircraft now being forced to withdraw to Aleppo; this base was too far to the rear to permit these aircraft to operate effectively over substantial parts of the front.

There had been several more encounters between the opposing fighters up to this time, particularly during the RAF's attacks on the French bases, and the D-520s had taken a further toll of the Hurricanes, though they had been mastered by the Tomahawks. Even as late as July 10th, when the French ground forces were in critical trouble, the D-520s could still make their presence felt, and on this date five Naval Dewoitines attacked twelve Blenheims of 45 Squadron from below when the bombers were near Hamma, shooting down three and damaging several more before escorting Tomahawks could get down to scatter the French fighters and claim all shot down. On the next day other D-520s strafed Palmyra airfield, destroying a number of British aircraft there, but strafing by the RAF was quickly reducing their numbers, and on July 12th all fighting ceased.

All remaining French aircraft and the majority of the military personnel elected to return to Metropolitan France, and with hostilities over most RAF units returned to Egypt. 127 Squadron was disbanded, the personnel forming the nucleus of a new 261 Squadron, and this unit, with 84 Squadron, remained to garrison the area.

By now Russia was in the war, and had become an ally, and in August British and Russian forces jointly moved into the oilfield area of Western Iran when the government of that nation failed to expel

c

Axis nationals. This short operation began on August 25th, and the army units taking part were supported by 261 Squadron with Hurricanes, 84 Squadron with Blenheims, and 244 Squadron with Vincents, together with a flight of 31 Squadron with Valentias. Strafing attacks on Iranian airfields in the area put an early end to any attempted interference from this quarter, one Iranian aircraft being shot down by 261 Squadron and others destroyed on the ground. By the 28th opposition had ended, and the eastern end of the Mediterranean could at last be considered secure. All efforts could now be concentrated on Libya and Malta.

The main activities in the Desert during the summer of 1941 surrounded the supply of the garrison in Tobruk, and many vicious fighter battles were fought over the convoys sailing between Alexandria and the fortress port. Fighter sweeps were also flown over the front, and heavily-escorted formations of bombers raided Axis airfields and supply lines.

At the same time both sides were slowly building-up their forces for the offensive which one or the other must sooner or later launch. 203 Squadron relinquished its Blenheim 4Fs in favour of Marylands for the general reconnaissance role over the Mediterranean, and 2 SAAF Squadron re-equipped with Tomahawks. 272 Squadron now went fully into action, making strafing attacks on communications and airfield targets of all sorts. During this period there were frequent combats over the front, losses on each side being about equal; Allied claims, however, were mainly against bombers, fighter-bombers and ground support aircraft, while their own losses were mainly fighters – victims of the ever dangerous Bf 109s. 250 Squadron engaged in a series of highly successful battles, Flg Off C.R. Caldwell especially beginning to run up a big score.

While the new build-up was just beginning, Collishaw, now an Air Vice-Marshal, left the Desert, his place as commander of 202 Group being taken by another old World War 1 warhorse, Air Vice-Marshal Sir Arthur 'Mary' Coningham. So far the limited number of units available in Egypt had generally prevented the grouping of squadrons into wings, but now in late July the first wing, 253, was formed with the special duty of giving close support to the ground forces. The wing was composite in nature, comprising 229 Squadron with Hurricane fighters, 113 Squadron with Blenheim 'strafers', and 451 Squadron, a new Australian unit, with Hurricanes for tactical reconnaissance. The wing was also at this stage mainly experimental, and its composite nature was not to last long.

In August 30 Squadron, now on Hurricanes, returned to operations as a night fighter unit, making a number of intruder sorties over the front after dark, and a few days later 112 Squadron also re-appeared in Egypt, now flying Tomahawks painted with a soon-to-be-familiar set of sharks' teeth on their noses. The Australian 3 RAAF Squadron soon joined 112, also with Tomahawks, following its successful activities over Syria, and a special formation, the Royal Naval Fighter Unit, comprising Hurricanes of 803 and 806 Squadrons and Grumman Martlets of 805 Squadron, was also set up to join the RAF in operations over the front from land bases. The bomber element was also reinforced by the arrival of 12 SAAF Squadron with Marylands. In the Delta area, defence rested with the Hurricanes of 213 Squadron.

Early in September the Italians, who had considerably reinforced their air units in Africa with more modern types, suddenly became aggressive, and launched a series of strafing attacks by fighters on Allied airfields in the Sidi Barrani area, very close to the front line. The first such attack on the 3rd was a failure as the Tomahawks of 2 SAAF Squadron were able to intercept the 27 Fiat G-50s carrying it out, and to shoot down six of them. However, on the 7th they met with considerably more success, no less than twenty-one British fighters being destroyed or badly damaged on the ground, and to prevent further such losses the RAF was forced to withdraw to airfields further back, in the Sidi Haneish area.

Throughout this period the Wellington squadrons in the Delta (now four in number) kept up regular night attacks on Benghazi, while the light bombers hammered away at targets just behind the front. In mid-September these activities intensified and three Blenheim squadrons, 11, 45 and 55, moved up to Fuka, while a third South African Maryland unit, 21 SAAF Squadron, also began operations. Following experience with 253 Wing, more wings were now forming, but grouping together squadrons of similar nature; initially it was intended that 258 Wing should undertake offensive action over Cyrenaica, 269 Wing should be responsible for interception of enemy aircraft over Egypt, and 262 Wing should protect the Delta and reinforce the other wings. In the event these specific functions did not remain for long, and when the offensive began all three wings were to operate over the front.

During October a second Gruppe of Bf 109s arrived in Africa, these being the vastly-improved F models. Although in the frequent clashes between Tomahawks and Bf 109Es, the RAF fighters had tended to come off rather worse, the performance of the Curtiss fighter was sufficiently high to worry the German pilots, and cause them to clamour for better aircraft; now they had them.

'Operation Crusader'

By this time the British ground forces, recently christened with the immortal name of the 8th Army, were approaching readiness for the new offensive, 'Operation Crusader', planned for mid-November; this was to be the biggest British offensive of the war so far. In a final flurry of reinforcements, five more Hurricane squadrons and one further Tomahawk unit moved into Egypt, including 80 Squadron, now the first RAF fighter-bomber unit, its Hurricanes being fitted to carry eight 40 lb bombs each; another Wellington squadron and several more Blenheim units, including a Free French squadron, also arrived, and a small detachment of four Boeing Fortress 1s reached the Delta from England to join the Wellingtons in their attacks on Benghazi.

Two photo-reconnaissance units, 2 PRU with Hurricanes and Beaufighters, and 60 SAAF Squadron with Marylands, were also now operating over Axis territory, and 24 SAAF Squadron was converting from Marylands to new Douglas Boston 3 bombers. On the eve of 'Operation Crusader' the greatly-strengthened RAF Order of Battle was as follows:

Fighters
258 Wing
1 SAAF, 94, 238 and 274 Squadrons	Hurricanes
2 SAAF and 3 RAAF Squadrons	Tomahawks

262 Wing
4 SAAF, 112 and 250 Squadrons	Tomahawks
80 Squadron	Hurribombers
229 and 260 Squadrons	Hurricanes

269 Wing
30 and 33 Squadrons	Hurricanes

Royal Naval Fighter Unit	Hurricanes and Martlets
272 Squadron (Detachment)	Beaufighters

Light Bombers

12 SAAF and 21 SAAF Squadrons	Marylands
24 SAAF Squadron	Bostons
8 (Detachment), 11, 14, 45, 55, 84 and 'Lorraine' Squadrons	Blenheims
113 Squadron	Blenheim 'strafers'

Heavy Bombers

37, 38, 70, 108, 148 Squadrons	Wellingtons
90 Squadron (Detachment)	Fortresses

General Reconnaissance

39 and 203 Squadrons	Marylands

Photographic Reconnaissance

2 PRU	Hurricanes and Beaufighters
60 SAAF Squadron	Marylands

On November 15th this considerable force opened an air offensive prior to the start of 'Operation Crusader', concentrating particularly on Axis airfields in an effort to win air superiority.

While the RAF had been growing rapidly into so formidable a force in Egypt, Malta too, had been playing its part. Throughout the summer and early autumn the Blenheims from the island went out at low level to interfere with the Axis attempts to build up their own forces in Africa. Each month the tonnage of shipping sunk increased, though losses suffered on these dangerous missions were frequently high. To make good attrition and increase the rate of attack more Blenheims were sent, the aircraft of 105 Squadron led by Wg Cdr Hughie Edwards, VC, DFC, flying in late in July and those of 107 Squadron a month later. At the same time 272 Squadron operated its Beaufighters from the island for a short period, attacking Libyan airfields in the Tripoli area in an effort to cut down the number of fighters available to intercept the Blenheims. 38 Squadron also moved in from Egypt, staying until mid-October, when Wellingtons of 40 and 104 Squadrons began arriving on the island from England.

The fighters were also far from idle; on July 26th a daring attempt was made by Italian 'E' Boats, escorted by Macchi 200 fighters, to penetrate Malta's Grand Harbour at Valetta. They were intercepted by Hurricanes of 126 and 185 Squadrons, some of them cannon-firing aircraft, and four 'E' Boats were destroyed, while three Macchis were shot down. Italian bombing raids were now rare, but the Macchis occasionally flew fighter sweeps over the island, and these usually resulted in spirited combats, four Macchis being claimed on August 19th, three on August 26th and four on September 4th, when two Hurricanes were also shot down.

Later in September the increased numbers of Blenheims available allowed regular raids on Sicilian airfields to be made, the bombers being escorted to and from the targets by Hurricanes. By mid-October the Hurricanes were themselves carrying bombs to drop on these targets. Late in September a supply convoy reached the island safely, 272's Beaufighters returning for six days to help escort it in, and a few days later the Blenheims of 18 Squadron arrived, releasing those of 105 Squadron, which returned to the United Kingdom. The Italians sprung one surprise on October 1st with the first appearance of their much-improved Macchi 202 fighter, powered by a German DB 601 engine. A number of these aircraft 'bounced' 185 Squadron and shot down the commanding officer, Sqn Ldr P. W. O. Mould, DFC. Generally, how-ever, the Italians appeared less than ever during this period, and combats during the hours of daylight became rare. At night the bombers attacked regularly, however, but the MNFU was now taking a regular toll, and during the night of October 14th Plt Off D. U. Barnwell shot down three raiders.

Early in November more Hurricanes were flown off *Argus* to Malta, these being aircraft of 242 Squadron. The Hurricane units had also received a new Wing Leader, Wg Cdr M. H. 'Hilly' Brown, an 'ace' of the Battles of France and Britain; unfortunately Brown failed to return from a sweep over Gela, Sicily, with 249 Squadron on November 12th. At this time the Blenheims redoubled their efforts to prevent Axis reinforcements and supplies reaching Africa as Operation 'Crusader' approached, but losses rose higher than ever, and on the 19th recently arrived 18 Squadron lost three in one mission. Late in the month the Macchis began appearing again and there were several dogfights, while reconnaissance aircraft of 69 Squadron experienced an increase in inter-ceptions, a Hurricane being lost on the 21st and a Maryland on the 24th.

At last all was ready in Egypt for the launching of 'Crusader'; the initial objective was to raise the siege of Tobruk and join up with the garrison there, the combined forces then turning to the second projected phase, the removal of Axis forces from Cyrenaica. The powerful mobile land forces were now supported by the greatly reinforced air force, now known as Western Desert Air Force, which had got fully into its stride during the recent months of stalemate. Even nature offered a helping hand, heavy rains during the night of November 17–18th turning the German fighter airfields at Gazala into a soggy morass.

The Axis had almost brought their own build-up to a climax, and were planning to launch a new assault on Tobruk only five days after the date set for 'Crusader'; when the British spearheads struck early on the 18th they were taken completely by surprise and little initial resistance was offered all along the front. Beaufighters of 272 Squadron were busy from the start, beginning a series of strafing attacks on Axis airfields during which many aircraft were to be destroyed on the ground. On the first day of the advance few enemy fighters were met, though one or two did manage to get into the air and shoot down two Marylands of 21 SAAF Squadron. Again on the 19th little opposition was met in the air, but on the ground 7th Armoured Brigade reached Sidi Rezegh, and 4th Armoured Brigade came up against 15th Panzer Division, battle then being joined in earnest.

Throughout the 20th the tanks battled, and activity in the air became much more violent, Tomahawks and Hurricanes undertaking continual patrols, escort and strafing missions throughout the day; during these, the aircraft of 80 Squadron undertook their first fighter-bombing sorties. 272 Squadron's Beaufighters had a particularly good day, arriving over a Stuka airfield in the Tmimi area as Ju 87s were landing and taking off, and quickly turning the busy scene into a charnel house. Four Ju 87s and a Fi 156 were shot down, 14 more Ju 87s and a lone Bf 109 being strafed on the ground and claimed destroyed. The worst blow to WDAF during the day occurred when a formation of unescorted Marylands following-in a fighter sweep over the front, were engaged by Bf 109s and lost four of their number.

During the day Rommel ordered 15th and 21st Panzer Divisions to disengage from their battle with the main British tank force and to move northwards to Sidi Rezegh where 7th Armoured Brigade and its Support Group were alone. Greatly outnumbered, the latter force was able to hold on until dusk, when 22nd Armoured Brigade arrived, but heavy losses were suffered.

In the air, the climax came on the 22nd when the German fighters launched a determined attempt to gain aerial superiority over the battlefield, and to drive the numerically-superior British fighters from the air. The first major clash came in the morning when Tomahawks of 3 RAAF Squadron escorted Blenheims of 45 Squadron over the front; four bombers and three Tomahawks failed to return. In the afternoon a Wing sweep by 112 and 3 RAAF Squadron was made over Tobruk and El Adem, Bf 109s intercepting and engaging in a classic dogfight which lasted for over an hour. When each side turned for home, seven more Tomahawks had gone down, and in the two battles only four Bf 109s had been claimed destroyed with four more probables. In fact six were lost, and though in this respect they were the victors, the Luftwaffe could not stand such a rate of loss to its slim fighter force. Clearly the British aircraft had the edge in manoeuvrability, and never again would the Germans directly challenge them in this way over Libya; in future they were content to rely upon the superior altitude performance of their aircraft to sit above the Allied formations and pick off aircraft at random. These tactics were to cause grievous losses to WDAF, but were to do little to prevent its units from carrying out their missions, and it can be said, therefore, that it was from this point that British air superiority over the Desert really began.

On the ground all was far from well, however, and having suffered heavy losses, the British armour was forced into retreat on the 23rd. An early morning attempt to dive-bomb the harassed forces was broken up by Hurricanes of 229 and 238 Squadrons, which claimed six Ju 87s and a fighter, but were badly cut-up by the escorts, losing seven aircraft, five from the latter unit alone.

Grasping his opportunity with both hands, Rommel now took the initiative, and on the 24th made a swift advance on the Egyptian frontier, overrunning the headquarters of XXX Corps in so doing. At night his columns passed close by Landing Ground 122 where 175 British aircraft were dispersed – fortunately without spotting them. Immediately this advance began all possible WDAF aircraft were put into the air to strafe the advancing panzers; while over the front 112 and 3 RAAF Squadrons engaged some seventy Axis aircraft supporting the drive, and shot down nine for the loss of two Tomahawks. At dawn next day the Germans struck at Sidi Aziez and Bir el Hariya, their tanks also rolling into Bardia. In an effort to stop the rot, the Tobruk garrison now sortied, reaching Ed Duda, while on the command level, General Cunningham was replaced as commander of the 8th Army by Major General Ritchie.

On the 27th the New Zealand Division recaptured Sidi Rezegh, and the Axis armour was forced to withdraw in the direction of Tobruk. The New Zealanders then reached Ed Duda, and the siege was broken for the first time in nearly eight months. The next day, however, the Axis force counter-attacked near Tobruk, again opening up a corridor between the port and Sidi Rezegh, and once more inflicting heavy losses on the battered 7th Armoured Division. On the 30th they made strong attacks on the Allied infantry at Sidi Rezegh, and by the end of the day the area was once more in their hands, Tobruk again being isolated.

During these crucial operations on the ground activity in the air continued at full scale; while Tomahawks swept the skies looking for the formations of Ju 87 and Ju 88 dive-bombers which frequently appeared during this period, Hurricanes strafed, bombed, and shepherded formations of Blenheims and Marylands to attack the columns of vehicles bringing up supplies for the Afrika Korps, and to bomb the airfields of the Luftwaffe and Regia Aeronautica. During the afternoon of the 28th Hurricanes of 94 Squadron were bounced by a lone Bf 109 while strafing and lost three of their number, but on the 30th the ubiquitous 112 and 3 RAAF Squadrons engaged fifty Axis aircraft over the front, claiming fifteen for the loss of three. On this occasion Wg Cdr Jeffrey landed to pick up Sgt 'Tiny' Cameron, a hulking six-foot Australian, and flew him back to base; one of the other pilots shot down during this combat was Plt Off Neville Duke, later famous as Hawker's Chief Test Pilot.

Rommel tried again on December 3rd, sending two columns towards the Egyptian frontier, but the air force was once more to the fore, strafing hard throughout the following day. The Luftwaffe was now becoming critically short of fuel, but the Ju 87s were thrown in again and again to try and help the panzers break through. The Allied fighters were ready for them, however, and on the 4th 112 and 2 SAAF Squadrons claimed seven of them, together with six escorting fighters, for the loss of two Tomahawks. The next day they did even better, 112 and 250 Squadrons claiming fifteen bombers and three fighters for the loss of five Tomahawks; on this occasion Flt Lt C. R. Caldwell of 250 Squadron personally accounted for five Ju 87s.

The Hurricanes were also frequently in combat and made regular claims, though not enjoying successes on the scale of the Tomahawks. They were, however, increasingly falling prey to the Bf 109s, and losses were heavy both to these and to ground fire as they pressed home their strafing attacks. On December 6th 229 and 238 Squadrons on a sweep over El Gubi encountered a small formation of Ju 87s and escorting fighters, and were joined by 274 Squadron which appeared in the area. However the bombers escaped, and while the Hurricanes were able to claim two of the escorts, they lost four of their own number. The next day other Hurricanes of 1 SAAF Squadron also attacked Ju 87s, but again could not get to them, losing three Hurricanes against claims for three escorting fighters. A little later 274 Squadron in the same area managed to shoot down one bomber, also claiming three escorts, but again three Hurricanes were lost.

Allied forces once more joined hands with the Tobruk garrison on December 8th, and the Afrika Korps, its bolt shot, drew back to prepared positions at Gazala during the next few days. As the now-tiring British forces prepared for the next phase, a new blow fell; news began to trickle through of the sudden Japanese attack on the Far Eastern possessions. It was at once clear that the diversion of supplies, reinforcements and units here could only be made at the expense of the Desert. Already new squadrons of Hurricanes destined for Africa were being redirected even while at sea, to this new front.

As the Afrika Korps withdrew to the Gazala line, air activity remained heavy, on the 9th alone four Tomahawks and seven Hurricanes being lost, but, undaunted, British fighter units now began moving to landing grounds nearer the front. The next day was one of tragedy for the SAAF; in the morning two Tomahawks were lost over the front, while in the afternoon six Bostons of 24 SAAF Squadron on only their second bombing sortie, were caught without escort, while relying on cloud cover for protection, and all but one were shot from the sky, the lone survivor limping back to base where it forcelanded. Before beginning bombing, these aircraft had flown a number of unescorted reconnaissance sorties, and had already suffered three losses while so engaged.

The other bomber units of the SAAF were not to escape either; on the 11th they were ordered to operate their Marylands as long-range fighters in an effort to intercept Ju 52 transport aircraft flying between Crete and the Desert with vital aviation fuel. Initially success greeted their efforts, three of the quarry being shot down, but to the great misgivings of the crews they were asked to repeat the exercise the next day, and this time five Marylands were shot down by escorting Bf 110s and Ju 88s; two Blenheims were also lost in the same area, though Beaufighters managed to shoot down one more Ju 52.

Apart from this diversion, most effort was made in support of the 4th Armoured Brigade, which was now attacking the Gazala positions; an early strafe by Hurricanes of 80 Squadron and the RNFU was intercepted, and four were shot down. 2 and 4 SAAF Squadrons then escorted bombers over the line, losing three Tomahawks, but claiming an equal number of their attackers. A little later other Tomahawks of

112 and 3 RAAF Squadrons swept the area, meeting many enemy aircraft, but claiming only two for the loss of four; 250 Squadron then repeated the sweep and redressed the balance, claiming two Ju 87s and two fighters.

Throughout the next three days the 8th Army battered at the Gazala line, finally on the 16th sending the 7th Armoured Division on an out-flanking move to the south. Although this threat was quickly bogged down in soft sand, it alarmed Rommel sufficiently to cause him to order a withdrawal, and by the 17th the Afrika Korps was in full flight. At once every aircraft was directed to attack the long and vulnerable columns and for three more days they strafed and bombed the unfortunate Germans and Italians throughout the hours of daylight.

The depredations of the striking force on Malta were now really being felt by the Axis, and shortage of fuel remained their most pressing and crippling problem. The Luftwaffe did what it could to protect the columns, but good though the results were, they were but a tiny proportion of what might have been achieved had they been able to put all their fighters into the air. On the 17th, the first full day of the retreat, Bf 109s caught Hurricanes of 1 SAAF Squadron escorting Blenheims, swooping down to shoot down four of the fighters and badly damage two more. On the 20th they badly broke up the formations of 112 and 250 Squadrons when the latter were engaged on similar duties, shooting down five Tomahawks and four of the Blenheims they were escorting, the British fighters being able to claim only three in return.

The true measure of the desperate fuel shortage can be gauged by the sheer numbers of aircraft the Axis were forced to abandon. During the rapid advance of mid-December, no less than 458 were counted on captured airfields, many still almost intact. On the 22nd Tomahawks attacked Magrun airfield when Ju 52s were flying in supplies of aviation fuel; large numbers of aircraft were caught on the ground and in the landing pattern, eleven, mainly Ju 87s and Ju 52s, being either shot down or burnt on the ground.

By now activity was over the Agedabia–Agheila area, the strafing and bombing sorties being carried out in the face of little opposition. 3 RAAF Squadron had been withdrawn on December 17th to re-equip with new Curtiss Kittyhawk fighters, developments of the Tomahawk with heavier armament and improved climbing performance, and the unit now returned to the front on the 27th to introduce these to action, 112 Squadron immediately flying back to Egypt to similarly equip. At this time, however, the new Far Eastern front took its toll, 45 and 113 Squadrons being withdrawn to fly their Blenheims out there, followed early in

January by 84 Squadron, and by 211 Squadron which had been acting as a Blenheim OTU in the Sudan.

After several quiet patrols, the Kittyhawks were blooded on New Year's Day, 1942, when the Australians met Ju 87s and their escorts, claiming four bombers and a fighter for a single loss. All was not well for the Allies, however, as on January 5th, 1942, a substantial Axis convoy reached Tripoli from Europe unscathed, the second in three weeks.

The reason for this was not hard to find; the effect of the constant attacks on convoys sailing between Europe and Africa by Malta-based aircraft had not gone unnoticed, and in mid-December a force of Ju 88s and Bf 109s was released from the Eastern Front and moved to Sicily to again undertake the subjugation of the island. Against these far-superior Bf 109Fs the Hurricanes of the defences were at a great disadvantage, and this was quickly made clear in the three days December 19th–21st when five Hurricanes were shot down by them. The British fighters also encountered difficulties in making any great impression on the fast and heavily-armoured Ju 88s, and the position on the island swiftly deteriorated.

On Christmas Day 21 Squadron's Blenheims arrived from England, and on January 4th others of 18 and 107 Squadrons made a successful and well-planned attack on Castel Vetrano airfield in Sicily, destroying a substantial number of aircraft on the ground. Such successes were now few and far between, however, and a few days later the remaining aircraft of these two units moved to Egypt, followed by the Wellingtons of 104 Squadron. Reinforcements were forthcoming, however, and so great was the island's need that Hurricanes of 605 Squadron on their way to the Far East were flown off an aircraft carrier to Malta instead.

At this stage the numbers of Luftwaffe aircraft involved in the new blitz were not vast, their effect resting more on their superior quality, but they were gradually added to, and when a convoy arrived in Grand Harbour on January 19th they were able to attack in force. By February the island's striking potential had sunk to practically nil, though the assorted Marylands, Beaufighters and Hurricanes of 69 Squadron continued to make their regular and important reconnaissance flights, suffering frequent losses while so doing.

In Libya, meanwhile, now with supplies to fall back on, and with his lines of communication shortening the whole time, Rommel withdrew his forces from the Agedabia area on January 6th before an Allied attack could be launched, and retreated to the Agheila line, a position of great natural strength. The arrival of supplies of fuel allowed the Luftwaffe to appear in force once more, and next day the Messerschmitts caught the two SAAF Tomahawk squadrons at a disadvantage and shot down seven, the South Africans being able to claim but two probables in return. 3 RAAF's Kittyhawks had more success on the 8th when they met an Italian formation, also back in the air, and claimed seven for no loss. Joined by 112 Squadron, now also Kittyhawk-mounted, the two units escorted Marylands over the front on the 9th but this time lost two of their new fighters to Bf 109s. Hurricanes of 229 Squadron on similar duty fared worse, losing four; no claims were made. Worse was to come; on the 14th 94 Squadron provided top cover to a Hurricane sweep and was 'bounced' by two Messerschmitts which shot down six of the unit's aircraft.

Despite these dashing victories, the Axis fighters were greatly outnumbered. At this time WDAF had 97 fighters at immediate readiness, with 25 more on 48 hours' call. Of 83 Bf 109s in Africa, only 26 were serviceable, and the number of modern Italian fighters able to take the air was even lower. Despite withdrawals to the Far East, the British could also call immediately on 28 bombers with another 28 ready at two days' notice.

British forces had entered Bardia on January 17th, and 'Crusader' had now reached its limit, the troops standing on much the same line as they had nearly a year earlier. At this stage several units, both ground and air, were withdrawn to re-equip, including the 7th Armoured Division and 12 and 21 SAAF Squadrons, which took the last of the Maryland bombers back to the Delta, though others remained in service in the general reconnaissance role. During the advance the RNFU had remained behind in the Tobruk area to patrol over supply convoys, but new units moved up towards the front; these were 40 SAAF Squadron, a tactical-reconnaissance unit, and GC III/2 *Alsace*, a French fighter squadron, both being equipped with Hurricanes. From England the radar-equipped Beaufighters of 89 Squadron arrived at Abu Sueir to provide the first effective night defence of the Delta.

Although the Axis forces were tired, Rommel now took one of the gambles for which he was to become so famous, and launched the Afrika Korps with less than sixty tanks and only two days rations, in a limited advance. As in March 1941 he took the British, weakened by the withdrawal of units for re-equipment, by complete surprise. The forward British airfields at Antelat had just been flooded by heavy rain, and WDAF was unable to interfere as the panzers sent XIII Corps reeling back to the Agedabia-El Haseit line. On the next day Antelat had dried out sufficiently to allow take-offs – very fortunately, as the fighters had to leave under fire from the advancing Axis forces and fly to Msus. Refuelled, Kittyhawks of 3 RAAF Squadron intercepted aircraft attacking the 1st Armoured Division and shot down three for the loss of two, all available fighters then being ordered once more to strafe the advancing columns.

The Hurricanes enjoyed a rare success on the 24th when six from 274 Squadron intercepted thirty Axis aircraft and claimed seven for one loss, but by the next day the surprised British forces were falling back all along the line. Convoys of coastal shipping were bringing supplies forward as fast as possible, and over one of these during the day, escorting Hurricanes shot down a total of four Ju 88s at various times, when these were making individual attacks.

On the 27th Rommel took a further gamble and sent a small column towards Mechili to give the impression that this was his main thrust, while in fact he swung the bulk of his forces northwards towards Benghazi. The bluff was a complete success, and the port was taken the next day, while on February 3rd Mechili was evacuated, and the Eighth Army began withdrawing to the Gazala line. By the 10th the Axis had reached Tmimi, and not possessing the force to storm the Gazala positions, they began constructing strong points; the Eighth Army was too weak to counter-attack, and the line quickly became static. A series of attempted outflanking moves by each side extended it further and further south until it petered out into the depths of the desert.

WDAF squadrons had withdrawn to Gazala on January 28th, and here at the end of the month a new RAAF Kittyhawk unit, 450 Squadron, arrived to reinforce them. 80 Squadron exchanged its decrepit Hurricane 1 bombers for newer Mark 2Cs, and 237 Squadron, relieved by the arrival of 40 SAAF Squadron, withdrew to rest. Operations during early February were concentrated mainly on strafing, but four days of heavy rain cut sorties considerably; on the 3rd 250 Squadron withdrew to get Kittyhawks, following 94 Squadron which had gone back to Egypt a few days earlier.

Activity in the air erupted again on the 8th as the Afrika Korps approached Tmimi, and eight Hurricanes of 1 SAAF Squadron were scrambled from Gazala, but were 'bounced' by two Bf 109s, two Hurricanes being shot down. 3 RAAF Squadron was then ordered to join 112 and 73 Squadrons, the latter newly returned to the front, for a mission over the lines. The Australian Kittyhawks were attacked as soon as they got into the air and two were shot down, in the event only one finally reaching the target area. In this vicinity 73 Squadron was then attacked, one Hurricane being lost, and 112 Squadron then fought a rearguard action, losing four Kittyhawks, but claiming three Bf 109s.

Four days later on February 12th Hurricanes of 73 and 274 Squadrons engaged Ju 87s and their escorts, claiming four victories against a loss of four fighters from the latter unit. On the 14th 112 and 3 RAAF Squadrons intercepted some thirty-two Ju 87s and MC 200s over Acroma, and claimed no less than twenty without loss, though it now seems that this was a considerable over-estimate. During the day 94 Squadron returned to Gazala with its new Kittyhawks, and a new commander, Sqn Ldr E. M. Mason, DFC, the top-scorer of the First Libyan Campaign. The next day the squadron joined 112 in a strafe of Martuba, but the formation was attacked by a lone Bf 109 flown by Oberfeldwebel Otto Schulz of II/JG 27, Mason and three other 94 Squadron pilots being shot down, while one 112 Squadron aircraft was badly damaged; 3 RAAF Squadron had already lost two Kittyhawks on this black day. Clearly, 94 was not really ready for operations, and it was at once withdrawn for further training; at the same time 260 Squadron also flew to Egypt to exchange its Hurricanes for Kittyhawks, while 30 Squadron began a series of moves which were to take it from the Mediterranean to the island of Ceylon, now threatened by the Japanese. Two new squadrons moved into the rear areas to do their final working-up before operating over the front, these being 335, a Greek squadron equipped with Hurricanes, and 5 SAAF, a new South African unit with Tomahawks.

The latter part of February was again plagued by bad weather, and air action was desultory, each side concentrating on strafing and bombing the other whenever possible; heavy clouds precluded the opportunity for much combat.

While little could be done at the front until strength had once again been built up, one constructive proposition offered itself: Malta's striking power could be revived to slow down Axis reinforcements and allow the Eighth Army to be ready for a new offensive first. In mid-February Beaufighters of 252 Squadron moved to Luqa to operate for a few days, but two were shot down as they prepared to return to Egypt on the 15th. The next day a number of new fighter pilots were flown in from England in a Sunderland, and on the 21st a detachment of six Wellingtons from 37 Squadron flew to the island from the Delta, followed by seven more on the next day. These efforts were to little avail as the Hurricanes could still not cope, and proved expensive in that virtually the whole Wellington detachment was wiped out on the ground during the next two weeks.

The next move came direct from England; Malta had to be held at all costs in the first instance, and as soon as possible it had to be in a position to resume offensive action. Consequently the first Spitfires to operate outside the United Kingdom (other than a few photographic-reconnaissance aircraft) were now put aboard the carrier *Eagle* and shipped out to the Mediterranean, being flown off to the island by replacement pilots for 249 Squadron on March 7th. They arrived only in the nick of time, for it was now that the last elements of the strike force disappeared, five Wellingtons being destroyed on the ground on the 9th and the remains of 21 Squadron being disbanded five days later.

The new Spitfires were first in action on the 10th, making their first claims, and soon they were hard at it, scrambling every day alongside the hard-pressed Hurricanes. They were very few in number at this time, and within a few days of arrival not more than half a dozen at best could be got into the air at any one time, but notwithstanding this, their arrival was a tonic to the defenders, who felt they were not forgotten.

On March 20th a new convoy approached the island, triggering off further heavy fighting as the Luftwaffe strove to destroy it; two ships managed to reach harbour and unload vital supplies. At this same time seven Beaufort torpedo-bombers of 22 Squadron arrived on their way to Egypt; one was shot down as it came in to land, but the others flew on to Africa the next day to add a new element to the strike capability there. Activity over the island remained hectic on the 21st as *Eagle* returned from Gibraltar with more Spitfires, this time for 126 Squadron. The Luftwaffe now launched a major assault, more than 300 bomber sorties being made on this day alone. A convoy from the opposite end of the Mediterranean fought its way through to the island on the 23rd, and on the 28th the air echelon of 229 Squadron flew in from Cyrenaica, followed the next day by more Spitfires launched from *Eagle* on her third trip. By the end of the month the defending fighters had claimed fifty-two bombers and seven fighters destroyed, but despite these losses to the enemy, fighting raged on unabated into April.

More Beauforts now arrived in Africa to replace 39 Squadron's Marylands, and on April 16th eight from 22 and 39 Squadrons, escorted by four Beaufighters of 272 Squadron took off to follow a Maryland of 203 Squadron leading them to an Axis convoy making for Tripoli. This was found under a heavy air umbrella of Sicily-based aircraft, and the Maryland, which was scouting ahead, was quickly shot down by a Ju

88. Two Bf 110s then attacked the Beauforts, but both were shot down by Sqn Ldr Riley of 272 Squadron; other fighters then joined in and two Beauforts were shot down. After launching their attack the remainder made for Malta, but two more were shot down within sight of the island and a fifth as it went in to land; the remaining aircraft landed, but all three were heavily damaged.

In the Desert there had been a considerable re-organization at the start of March, 258 and 262 Wings being renumbered 243 and 239 respectively, while a third wing, 233, was formed, these now forming a new Group, 211. The composition of the wings was as follows: 239 Wing : 3 RAAF, 112, 250, 450 Squadrons – Kittyhawks; 243 Wing : 33, 73, 80, 274 Squadrons – Hurricanes; 233 Wing : 2 SAAF, 4 SAAF, 94, 260 Squadrons – Kittyhawks and Tomahawks.

The first half of March was marked by very bad weather and frequent storms which greatly reduced activity in the air, but on the night of the 2nd–3rd 89 Squadron gained the first radar-guided night victories for the RAF in the Mediterranean, when two He 111s were shot down over Alexandria. Better weather on the 8th brought out 239 Wing, 3 RAAF and 450 Squadrons intercepting a large formation of Ju 87s and Italian fighters, claiming two of the former and seven of the latter for no loss. The enemy formation then fell foul of 112 Squadron which claimed two more.

Over a convoy moving up the coast on March 11th three patrolling Beaufighters of 252 Squadron shot down six attacking bombers, three falling to Flg Off H. H. K. Gunnis, and over the front the return of reasonable weather conditions gave rise to regular skirmishes between the opposing fighters, RAF attrition during these remaining definitely on the high side. On April 6th the Afrika Korps moved forward to consolidate around Sidi Breghix and Segnali, this leading to a further outbreak of heavy fighting on the ground.

April thereafter remained unexceptional until the 25th, when all four squadrons of 233 Wing scrambled to intercept Ju 87s and escorting Bf 109s. While claiming two bombers and three fighters, the Wing suffered heavily, eight fighters being shot down or crash-landing, while two more were badly damaged. A promising event occurred five days later, however, with the arrival at Helwan of 145 Squadron with Spitfire 5Cs, the first Spitfire unit to reach the Desert.

Other more modern equipment was also at last arriving, and 108 Squadron in the Delta began augmenting its Wellingtons with some Consolidated Liberator 2 four-engined bombers. 208 Squadron now returned to the front, equipped with two flights of Hurricanes and one of Tomahawks for tactical reconnaissance work; 40 SAAF Squadron had also received a number of Tomahawks to augment its Hurricanes on these duties by this time.

The weather again turned bad in early May, and on the 10th came a shock for 94 Squadron when it was ordered to hand its Kittyhawks to 2 SAAF Squadron and its more experienced pilots to 260 Squadron, and withdraw to the Delta to re-equip with Hurricanes for rear area defence duties.

In Cyrenaica both sides were fast approaching the time when they could again launch an offensive, and the Luftwaffe too had been receiving reinforcements from Sicily. The WDAF was still suffering frequent combat losses, particularly to tactical reconnaissance aircraft, and to fighters on bomber escort duties over the front. New units were now arriving fast, most being used to relieve those existing squadrons in rear areas so that they could move up to the front; these new arrivals included 7 SAAF, 134 and 417 (RCAF) Hurricane Squadrons, and 92 Squadron. This latter unit was another Spitfire squadron from the United Kingdom, but it had arrived without its aircraft and was consequently of little initial use. 46 Squadron, the nucleus of which had been in Egypt for many months, was now working up as the second Beaufighter night-fighter unit, 6 Squadron was re-equipping with Hurricane 2Ds which carried a pair of 40mm anti-tank guns beneath the wings, and 55 and 223 Squadrons were receiving a new light bomber, the Martin Baltimore, a development of the Maryland, designed specially to British requirements.

In the midst of all this activity a special mission was laid on; it was known that supply Ju 52s were again shuttling between Crete and Benghazi, and in an effort to intercept these six Beaufighters of 252 Squadron and ten Kittyhawks of 250 Squadron were sent out on May 12th, meeting fourteen of the transports and two Bf 110s. The British fighters attacked at once, claiming fifteen Ju 52s (actual loss nine) and both Bf 110s; the latter and two of the Junkers were all claimed by Flg Off J. D. Waddy of 250 Squadron. One Beaufighter was shot down by return fire, but all other aircraft returned from this very successful operation.

Malta received further reinforcements late in April with the arrival of the pilots and aircraft of 601 and 603 Squadrons, flown off the US carrier *Wasp* on the 20th. Their arrival instituted violent German reaction, both on the day of their arrival, and on the following day when no less than 325 bomber sorties were made over the island. In a very short time a considerable number of the new Spitfires had been destroyed on the ground. An attempt was then made to hit the Luftwaffe on its own landing grounds in Sicily, and for this purpose ten Wellingtons arrived from Egypt on the 26th. The next day six were destroyed in their pens on the ground, and when the four survivors operated over Sicily that night, two were shot down; the final pair returned to Africa next morning.

Early May saw two innovations; firstly all ground crews were issued with rifles so that they could hit back at the Luftwaffe aircraft continually over their bases, and secondly, for the first time in several months, Italian fighters again appeared over the island. *Wasp* now began a second journey through the Mediterranean to deliver more Spitfires, and this time very careful and well-organized preparations were made for their arrival on the 9th. With ground crews ready to refuel and re-arm the aircraft immediately on arrival, and pilots ready to take them over from the new arrivals and, with Malta's existing fighter force patrolling overhead, the new aircraft were this time received and ready for action with very few losses, despite determined German attacks.

Accompanying *Wasp* was another convoy, which now tried desperately to get through, but ship after ship was sunk until on the 10th only the tanker *Welshman* limped into harbour. The new strength of the defences was able to make itself felt on this day, however, sixteen confirmed and twenty probable victories being claimed by the Spitfires and eight by the guns. The scores of several pilots on the island were growing fast at this time, but on May 18th Plt Off P. A. Nash, one of the first Spitfire pilots to arrive, and victor of ten and a half combats over the island, was killed. At this stage still more Spitfires were flown off to Malta, this time from *Eagle*, and the defence was now becoming a force to be reckoned with. Ten more Wellingtons were now sent in, and though two crashed into craters on arrival, the remainder were able to fly a number of raids over Sicily and southern Italy. Spitfires were being poured into Gibraltar for delivery now, and *Eagle* was back on June 3rd, flying off twelve more; Bf 109s from Pantelleria intercepted them on the way and shot down four, but on the 9th *Eagle* flew off another thirty-two. Meanwhile these reinforcements led to the withdrawal to Egypt of the remnants of 229 Squadron, this unit then being disbanded. The Wellingtons also flew back to Egypt to leave room on the island for Royal Navy torpedo-bombers.

In the Desert late in May it became obvious that something was afoot, as Axis air activity began to increase. On the 23rd the new Baltimores of 223 Squadron were dispatched on their first mission over the front, a formation of four setting off without fighter escort. Inevitably, they were engaged by Bf 109s and three were shot down, the fourth being so badly damaged that it crash-landed before it could regain its own base; almost all the rear-firing armament failed during the combat, and all aircraft had to be modified before they could go out again. They were not, however, to be sent out again without adequate fighter escort – the lesson had at last been learned.

As a new Axis attack was obviously pending, 145 Squadron with its Spitfire 5s was sent forward to Gambut on the 24th to begin operations, but at this time the WDAF lost Sqn Ldr Caldwell, who finished his tour with twenty and a half victories to his credit as top-scorer to date with the RAF in the Desert. During the night of the 25th a heavy raid was launched by the Luftwaffe on Landing Ground 143 at Gasr el Arid, four German bombers being shot down, three by the night-flying Hurricanes of 73 Squadron, recently converted from day operations. Next day Rommel's new offensive began with an attack by Italian infantry and artillery on the heavily-fortified Allied line to the north, while armoured columns of the Afrika Korps by-passed the outlying defences at Bir Hakeim to the south and swinging north-eastwards, made for Acroma and El Adem. At the same time the Axis air forces launched a series of violent assaults on Allied landing grounds, and very heavy fighting ensued, Ju 87s once more appearing in numbers, always with heavy fighter escorts.

The Axis armour reached an area known to the British as Knightsbridge on the 27th, and here a great tank battle began which was to last for several days. The next day the army commander asked the RAF to cut air superiority operations and throw all possible aircraft into the ground attack role in support of the army, in an effort to cut the enemy's supply lines and halt his advance. The critical situation on the ground warranted such a decision, but was to leave the Allied squadrons open to the depredations of the marauding Axis fighters, and losses rose steeply in consequence. The fighting grew even more desperate on the 30th when bombers and fighter-bombers poured in a steady stream to the scene of the battle – known as 'The Cauldron'. The dedication of the escorts preventing the enemy fighters from getting through to the light bombers on the majority of occasions, but this was only achieved at great cost, and little could be done to cover the fighter-bombers. By the end of the month thirty-nine fighters and fighter-bombers had been lost in three days, with many others damaged, but sandstorms then enforced a brief reduction in the numbers of operations flown.

On June 1st the first Spitfire sorties were made, and on the 2nd Italian forces, heavily supported by Ju 87s, attacked the Free French positions at Bir Hacheim to remove the threat posed by them to the Afrika Korps' left flank.

At once every available Allied aircraft was diverted to assist the French to repel this new threat, and a number of violent new combats occurred. Over the French positions on June 3rd Tomahawks of 5 SAAF Squadron claimed no less than eight Ju 87s shot down, but while their attention was so diverted they were attacked from behind by Oberleutnant Hans-Joachim Marseille of I/JG 27, who shot down five of the South African aircraft and damaged a sixth so badly that it force-landed as it returned to base. Next day 4 and 5 SAAF Squadrons were again over Bir Hakeim, claiming six more Stukas, but again five Tomahawks were lost. Pilots were now regularly flying three or four sorties a day, and as nightfall came the French commander signalled *'Bravo! Merci pour le RAF!'*; *'Bravo à vous!'* came the reply, *'Merci pour le sport!'*

Torn between two vital areas, the fighter-bombers were back over Knightsbridge on June 6th, Kittyhawks claiming to have destroyed some seventy vehicles during the day, and it was in this area that the Hurricane 2D 'tank-busters' first put their 40 mm cannon-armament into action on the 7th. More squadrons were rushed forward from the Delta, 213 Squadron joining 73 Squadron – temporarily back on day operations – in throwing their Hurricanes into the fray on the 8th, when the air force was again directed to Bir Hakeim. Here on the 9th three more large Stuka attacks developed, causing heavy and confused fighting with substantial losses on both sides. With the Free French cut off from supply columns on the ground, Bombays of 216 Squadron flew in vital stores at night.

The responsibilities of the RAF were further stretched on June 11th when a supply convoy put out from Alexandria to approach Malta from the east, while a second convoy sailed from Gibraltar in the west. The latter was beyond the range of Africa-based Allied units, and was covered by carrier aircraft of the Royal Navy, but the former relied for its air cover on the squadrons in Egypt and Libya. The prolonged resistance at Bir Hakeim, however, had completely upset Rommel's time-table, and at this stage the battle was very much in the balance. The 13th was to be the decisive day, when the Afrika Korps' 90th Light Division attacked and captured El Adem, British armour at Knightsbridge suffering heavy losses and being driven back towards the coast; sandstorms prevented WDAF from taking much part in these moves.

On June 14th a general retreat from the Gazala area began, and squadrons started a series of 'leapfrogging' moves to landing grounds further east. In the air, however, the main centre of activity shifted northwards to the area of sea between Crete and Africa, known as 'Bomb Alley', where the convoy from Alexandria was under heavy attack by aircraft from both Cretan and Cyrenaican bases. Kittyhawks and Beaufighters were sent out to patrol over the convoy, where they became involved in almost continual combats with all types of Axis aircraft, 272 Squadron alone losing five Beaufighters on this date. Later in the day a substantial Italian naval force was spotted, including capital ships, and at dusk torpedo aircraft were sent out from Malta to attack.

More attacks on the hard-pressed convoy were made on the 15th by SM 79s and Ju 87s, on one occasion Kittyhawks and Beaufighters intercepting nine torpedo-carrying SM 79s and driving them off less two of their number. Meanwhile two Allied formations set out from Egypt to seek the Italian fleet; Beauforts of 39 Squadron escorted by Beaufighters of 272 Squadron were intercepted by Bf 109s while *en route* to their targets, three Beauforts and two of the escort being shot down, while four more bombers were damaged so badly that they had to turn back. The remaining five launched their torpedoes at the enemy ships at the same time as a formation composed of two Liberators of 160 Squadron, which had just arrived from England, and seven B-24s of the newly-arrived Halvorsen Detachment (the first American unit to reach the Middle East) bombed from higher up. Resistance was too strong for the convoy, however, and with the Italian fleet at sea it turned back next day. The other convoy from Gibraltar had approached Malta on the 14th, and came within range of the island's aircraft, which had been reinforced by the Beaufighters of 235 Squadron from England. Despite all efforts of the defenders, the convoy was subjected to violent air attack, and finally on the 16th, the day on which the Alexandria convoy turned back, just two ships managed to enter harbour.

At the same time the situation in the Desert worsened; on June 15th Rommel turned his spearheads due east and struck for Sidi Rezegh, nearly reaching this point the next day and pressing on to Belhamed. Again the air force was thrown in to try and stem the tide, and all units were flat out, operations reaching a crescendo on the 17th. During this latter day fighters escorting formations of Bostons over the front were 'bounced' on several occasions, and lost ten of their number. During this fighting Sgt J. Dodds of 274 Squadron claimed his fourteenth victory; all gained in the space of a few months, this score made him by far the most successful Hurricane pilot on this, or any other front during 1942.

The Luftwaffe was moving up fast in the wake of the advancing Afrika Korps, and during the 17th substantial numbers of Bf 109s arrived at Gazala. An immediate raid by the Kittyhawks of 239 Wing was laid on during the afternoon, and fifteen fighters were strafed on the ground. During the evening all British fighter units withdrew to the Sidi Aziez area, and the increased range, together with the lessening of ground fighting as the Allied retreat got fully under way, caused a drop in aerial activity.

As the Allied forces moved back into Egypt, General Auchinleck had determined that this time there would not be a long siege of Tobruk, as the supply of the large garrison necessary to hold the port laid too great a burden on the supply services, and slowed down the build-up necessary for a counter-offensive. Consequently, on the 21st the defenders of the port surrendered – an act which was to cause a profound shock to the Allied nations, and badly affect morale. With this success, Rommel changed his plans, which had been to halt on the Egyptian frontier while an invasion of Malta was launched to secure his supply lines, and he now decided to push on in the hope of reaching the Suez Canal. On June 24th his forces crossed the frontier into Egypt.

It was at this juncture that General Auchinleck took over direct command of the 8th Army from General Ritchie. Despite the loss of some 60,000 men, the Army had not disintegrated, mainly thanks to the air support afforded it, and remained a cohesive unit. Auchinleck at once began to develop the defences of a line situated at the narrowest point between the Mediterranean and the virtually impassable Qattara Depression, a line running south from the rail halt of El Alamein.

The RAF by now had moved back to the Sidi Haneish area, where it was reinforced by the arrival of 601 Squadron from Malta with Spitfire 5s, 127 and 335 Squadrons with Hurricane 2s, and the new South African unit, 7 SAAF Squadron, which was to operate Hurricane 1s as fighter-bombers. German fighters moved up to Sidi Barrani on June 25th, and with this stabilization of the front, the opposing air forces once more clashed violently on the 26th. So effective was the continual Allied air offensive that by late afternoon the Axis columns had been brought to a halt by the sustained attack, but the cost was again high, the Messerschmitts taking a dreadful toll, including Sqn Ldr A. W. Barr, DFC, commanding officer of 3 RAAF Squadron, who had over twelve victories to his credit, and who was forced to bale out of his burning Kittyhawk to become a prisoner of war.

There was less activity on the 28th, although 238 Squadron was badly 'bounced' and lost six Hurricanes. Despite the alarming rate of fighter losses, the enemy was still being prevented from getting through to the all-important bombers, and indeed so effective were the Kittyhawks and Tomahawks of 233 Wing in the escort role that during the first twenty-three days of the Axis offensive not one bomber in their care was lost to aerial attack. The night bombers however were not being so lucky; the Germans had now moved a number of Ju 88 nightfighters to Africa from Europe for the defence of the main ports, and Wellingtons from the Delta were now suffering regular and increasing losses to these nocturnal predators.

By the end of June the 8th Army was firmly entrenched on the Alamein line, while the Axis were tired, weakened, and short of supplies. The WDAF was being further reinforced ready for the next round, and the first of several USAAF units were arriving in the area. A number of four-engined Handley Page Halifax bombers, flown out from England, were formed into two composite squadrons, while the pilots of 92 Squadron, still awaiting their Spitfires, were temporarily attached to 80 Squadron to fly Hurricanes.

Hoping to continue his advance with the forces still available to him, Rommel launched an attack on the Alamein line on July 1st, and this again led to heavy fighting in the air. On the 3rd Ju 87 formations were twice intercepted by Hurricanes and suffered heavy losses, the fighter squadrons involved being 33, 73 and 1 SAAF; the South Africans alone claimed thirteen of the dive-bombers shot down. The next day the Stukas were again intercepted on a number of occasions and several more were destroyed. On the ground the Afrika Korps was making no progress, and the attack was then called off, the Axis forces going on to the defensive for the time being.

In support of Rommel's drive on Egypt, the Axis air forces in Sicily launched a new assault on Malta on July 1st, and during the next few days the island was once more fighting for its very existence. The Spitfires were continually in the air, and by the 14th had claimed forty-four attacking aircraft shot down, of which thirty-three were bombers. The defenders own losses were serious, totalling no less than thirty-nine fighters, but twenty-six of the pilots were saved, and most were able to return to the fray. Losses were quickly made good when thirty-two new Spitfires were flown in from *Eagle*, and at this time command of the island's air force was taken over from Air Vice-Marshal H. P. Lloyd by Air Vice-Marshal Sir Keith Park who had so ably commanded the vital

11 Group of Fighter Command during the Battle of Britain just two years earlier.

Following the violent 'blitz' of the first fortnight of July, the second half of the month was much quieter. Late in the month 603 Squadron, which had never been joined by its ground echelon, was disbanded, the pilots and aircraft being used as the nucleii of two new squadrons; the old night fighter flight, numbered 1435 Flight during the earlier part of the year, had ceased to be necessary after the arrival late in June of a flight of Beaufighters of 89 Squadron from Egypt, and the number was now given to one of the new squadrons, while 229 Squadron was reformed as the other.

In Egypt Allied tactical bombing was now becoming a polished art. During recent operations 233 Wing had concentrated on escort missions to the Bostons, of 12 SAAF and 24 SAAF Squadrons, while 239 Wing specialized in fighter-bomber activities. The return to operational flying of the Baltimore squadrons, 55 and 223, led to the need for more escorts, however, and 239 Wing now began to fly a number of such missions escorting these aircraft. While the Hurricanes were retained to a large extent to combat the Ju 87s, with which they could well cope, the Spitfires operated high over the battlefield, giving cover to all the other types, and to some extent neutralizing the high-flying activities of the Bf 109s, so far as the still limited numbers of these British fighters allowed. Tight, imperturbable formations of nine, twelve or eighteen Bostons or Baltimores, heavily escorted by a swarm of Kittyhawks and Tomahawks, now became a familiar sight as they passed regularly over the front to hammer at Axis supply lines, dumps and troop concentrations. During July also, 21 SAAF Squadron returned to action with 3 SAAF Wing, flying Baltimores; at this time too, a new fighter wing, 7 SAAF Wing, was formed, initially comprising 33, 73 and 7 SAAF Squadrons. 4 SAAF Squadron in 233 Wing had by now fully re-equipped with Kittyhawks.

During mid-July several local Allied attacks were launched to consolidate the hastily-prepared positions, and in each case these led to heavy fighting both on the ground and in the air. With Crete now in easy flying distance of forward German airfields, its use as a staging post to fly in urgent supplies and reinforcements again came to the fore, and Beaufighters were sent out on patrol trying to catch the Ju 52s over the sea.

Recent operations had left the Afrika Korps with only twenty-eight serviceable tanks, and on July 19th Rommel ordered these to be dug in, in defensive positions. This move was taken in the nick of time, as two days later Auchinleck launched a counter-attack in force with newly re-equipped units, in an effort to drive the Axis forces back to the Egyptian frontier. The advancing columns fell foul of the German defences on the 20th, losing forty tanks of a hundred employed, against a minimal loss of three. The fighting was, of course, accompanied by greatly increased activity in the air, but the offensive was ill-fated, making little progress during the next few days, and by the 23rd tank losses had risen to 118. The next day, while the opposing air forces clashed violently overhead, it was brought to a halt, and by the 27th it was all over, the forces having withdrawn behind the Alamein line. There was then a lull, as each side hurried to push forward supplies and more new equipment.

Early August on Malta was as quiet as late July, but action was again brewing, as a large new convoy, this time escorted by a substantial naval force including four aircraft carriers, was preparing to make the run across the Western Mediterranean; the operation was codenamed 'Pedestal'. To assist in reconnaissance which would be vital to such an undertaking, a number of Baltimores were flown to the island to supplement 69 Squadron's Marylands and Hurricanes, while sixteen Beaufighters of 248 Squadron were flown out from England, and another half-dozen were sent from 252 Squadron in Egypt to attack Axis airfields from which raids on the convoy would be launched.

As the convoy approached under an effective Royal Navy fighter umbrella, the Beaufighters went out on August 11th to strafe airfields in Sardinia. The next day the convoy came within range of Malta-based aircraft, Beaufighters being sent out first to escort the merchant vessels as the carriers turned for the return run to Gibraltar, Spitfires following later in the day as the range closed. Very heavy Axis air attacks were made on the 13th, a day of much combat, but sufficient vessels got through to keep the defenders going, and on the 14th the attacks tailed off.

Following the arrival of the survivors of the convoy, the Beaufighters of 235 and 248 Squadrons still remaining on the island were combined to form a new squadron, 227. Joined by the Beauforts of 39 Squadron, which had just been re-formed from the remnants of 86, 217, and the old 39 Squadrons, they then began a series of strikes on Axis shipping plying between Sicily and Africa. The cessation for the time being of Axis raids on the island allowed the use of the Spitfires in an offensive manner for the first time, and a series of sweeps over southern Sicily began. Most of these failed to cause any reaction on a large scale, but on August 27th a sweep resulted in a considerable number of combats, and in the loss of a veteran fighter pilot, Gp Capt W. M. Churchill, DFC, whose Spitfire was shot down by flak. This new offensive capability of the island's forces was extended to the hours of darkness when 69 Squadron took on charge a number of torpedo-carrying Wellingtons for operations by one flight.

August in the Desert had also been fairly quiet. The main event had been the complete change-over in the army high-command; on August 7th Lt-Gen Gott had been on his way to take command of the Eighth Army when the 216 Squadron Bombay in which he was a passenger was intercepted and shot down by Bf 109s, the General losing his life. He was replaced by Lt-Gen Bernard Montgomery, and on the 15th Auchinleck was relieved as commander-in-chief by Gen Sir Harold Alexander. These two able new leaders at once began a command shake-up throughout the Eighth Army.

In the air 92 Squadron had at last received its Spitfires, and the first American P-40F Warhawks of the US 57th Fighter Group were also appearing over the front; both units were to make their first claims in Africa on August 14th. Other American units with B-24 heavy bombers and B-25 mediums were also arriving, and would soon join the fray. On the debit side the Free French fighter unit, GC III/2 *Alsace* after several weeks action during the Gazala battles, now handed in its Hurricanes and left to re-form in the United Kingdom. 14 Squadron, the last unit still flying Blenheims, also withdrew after several months of night operations, to re-equip with new Martin Marauder bombers.

As always, shipping carrying supplies for Rommel's forces from Sicily to Benghazi, Tripoli and Tobruk remained a priority target. A Hudson squadron, 459, had been formed from predominantly RAAF personnel earlier in 1942 for anti-shipping operations, but had suffered heavy casualties recently, losing four aircraft during the first fortnight of August while making low level attacks on enemy supply vessels. Its duties were now made a little easier by the arrival in Egypt of 15 SAAF Squadron, equipped with Bisleys (Blenheim 5s) specifically for operations against coastal shipping in co-operation with Beaufighters. Throughout this period Allied fighter escorts and fighter-bombers were still regularly attacked by Axis fighters, and losses were frequent, but at night the picture was much improved following the withdrawal to Europe of the majority of the German night-fighters.

A small side-light at this time was the activities of a few specially modified Spitfires, flown by pilots of 103 Maintenance Unit. The

Germans had sent to Africa a small number of Ju 86P reconnaissance aircraft, which were fully pressurized and could fly at very high altitude. So far these aircraft had been able to operate over Alexandria and the Delta virtually unchallenged. A pair of Spitfires were stripped of every conceivable item, and were modified to give optimum performance at high altitude; several abortive attempts at interception culminated on August 24th when Flg Off Reynold finally managed to catch one of the Ju 86Ps above 40,000 feet and shoot it down.

Rommel had now received sufficient forces to attempt a new assault, and during the night of August 30th–31st the Afrika Korps began moving up to attack the Allies at Alam el Halfa, at the southern end of the line, in an attempt to turn Montgomery's left flank. The new commander had anticipated this move, however, and had concentrated a substantial force here, with his tanks dug in in strong defensive positions. At dawn on the 31st the Germans attacked, supported by attacks by large formations of Ju 87s, and heavy fighting on the ground and in the air began again. WDAF was thrown in, making an all-out assault on the Axis columns with every available aircraft, though the Messerschmitts were much in evidence, and eight fighters were lost.

The next day twenty more failed to return and many others were badly damaged; it is sobering to note that at least a dozen of the aircraft lost were shot down by one man, Hauptmann Marseille. Despite these losses the fighters did their job magnificently, and throughout the day not one bomber was lost to Axis fighters, the operations of the Afrika Korps being very seriously restricted and disrupted by the continual aerial bombardment. These activities continued unabated during the next day, when Axis ground forces were able to make little headway, and on this day fighter losses dropped to ten. On September 3rd the British counter-attacked, forcing the Axis into retreat, and 200 bomber sorties were flown without loss, though the fighters again suffered severely, typified by 7 SAAF Squadron which lost four aircraft in one mission. In the four days fighting WDAF lost 13 bombers with 13 more damaged, nearly all to ground fire, and 43 fighters (17 of them Hurricanes) with 27 badly damaged, the majority of these losses being to the enemy fighters. On September 4th, when there was a great reduction in the level of activity, Rommel decided to withdraw, mainly due to the disruption and loss of vehicles caused by air attack, and by the 5th the front was quiet again.

Despite this rebuff, the German fighters were still about, and were able once more to inflict serious losses on the Allied formations on September 6th. 7 SAAF Wing still included 7 SAAF Squadron, but the

RAF squadrons now with it were 6, 127 and 274. On this date 127, 274 and 7 SAAF Squadrons undertook a wing fighter-bomber operation during which they were bounced by Bf 109s, losing eight Hurricanes, five of them from the SAAF unit which had only one aircraft return from this mission. So heavy had been the losses suffered by this squadron in recent weeks that it had to be withdrawn from the front on the 9th.

As the Eighth Army now concentrated on building-up for a new Allied offensive, all efforts in the air were aimed at preventing or slowing down a similar build-up by the Axis. One facet of this was a series of formation daylight raids on Crete by heavy bombers; the two composite squadrons of Halifaxes were now concentrated into one squadron, 462, and with the Liberators of 160 Squadron and the American B-24s, these fought their own little war over the island with defending Bf 109s, 110s and Ju 88s, while they bombed harbours and airfields.

Over the front raids continued, Allied medium and light bombers flying westwards, while formations of Stukas flew the other way to hammer the British front line positions. Beaufighters were very active along the coast of Africa, and at night the Wellingtons kept up their attacks on Axis ports. Newer aircraft, Kittyhawk 3s and Baltimore 3s, were beginning to reach the squadrons, and two American P-40 squadrons from the 57th Fighter Group were now attached, one to each of the Kittyhawk wings, to gain operational experience. The first Canadian squadron in the Middle East, 417, was now equipped with Hurricanes for the defence of Suez, while 7 SAAF Squadron began re-equipping as the second Hurricane 2D 'tank-buster' unit.

The Beaufighters of 252 Squadron undertook two missions of a different nature on October 6th and 7th when they carried out strafing attacks on an Italian seaplane base at Menelais Bay, Crete, hitting a number of aircraft riding at anchor. A great opportunity was offered on October 9th when air reconnaissance noted that the main Axis forward landing grounds at Daba and Fuka were waterlogged following recent heavy rains, and an immediate assault was thrown in, seven bombing raids being sent over, together with numerous fighter-bomber attacks. Despite the state of the airfields, substantial numbers of defending fighters managed to get into the air, and some very heavy fighting ensued as Baltimores, Bostons, B-25s, Hurricanes, Kittyhawks, Tomahawks, Spitfires and P-40s converged on the area in a series of strikes collectively known afterwards as the 'Daba Prang'. Whether the results justified this massive effort is highly questionable; fifty aircraft were claimed destroyed on the ground and ten shot down, for a loss of at least fifteen fighters and one bomber, with others badly damaged. Actual losses on the ground totalled ten aircraft destroyed and twenty damaged; the claims in the air were relatively accurate.

On Malta during September and early October all had been very quiet, few enemy aircraft being seen and only the odd 'scramble' being ordered. Beaufighters, Beauforts, Wellingtons and Royal Navy Albacores kept up their attacks on the Axis seaborne supply lines, inflicting most damaging losses in Italian shipping tonnage; meanwhile, the Spitfire squadrons continued their offensive sweeps over Sicily, and 126 Squadron began dropping bombs from improvised bomb racks, apparently the first Spitfire squadron so to do.

The continual attacks on Rommel's supplies were having a most deleterious effect on the Afrika Korps, which was being slowly strangled by lack of fuel and other vital items. In desperation another 'blitz' on the island was launched on October 11th, and at once the air between Malta and Sicily was a mass of combats. This time, however, there were five full squadrons of Spitfires available, and they were able to meet the attackers in strength, quickly gaining the upper hand. For seven days the fighting continued with unabated fury, but by then the losses of Ju 88 bombers had been so catastrophic that Kesselring, the Luftwaffe commander, was forced to order them to cease daylight operations. This was a major victory for the defenders who had claimed more than forty of the bombers shot down during this week of combat, together with about fifty of the German and Italian fighters escorting them.

RAF losses had not been light, but many pilots were saved, including Flg Off G. F. Beurling, DSO, DFC, DFM, who was shot down and wounded after gaining his twenty-sixth victory over the island; a New Zealander Plt Off N. M. Park, was, however, killed after claiming eight victories. For several days after the withdrawal of the bombers, formations of Axis fighters flew sweeps towards the island, and defending Spitfires frequently clashed with them, but the weight had gone out of the attack, these sweeps gradually petering out. Losses of aircraft were made good once more when a new batch of Spitfires flew in on October 24th.

The Battle of El Alamein

Operations over the Desert during mid-October had been considerably curtailed by sandstorms, but on the 19th WDAF opened a new air offensive as a prelude to the forthcoming new offensive on the ground, attacking Axis positions and lines of communication in Egypt, while Beaufighters redoubled their efforts to catch the elusive Ju 52s between Crete and the mainland; they did succeed over the next few days in intercepting and shooting down several.

A second big series of attacks on the Daba landing grounds was made on October 20th, eleven enemy aircraft being shot down, with two more destroyed and fifteen damaged on the ground, for the loss of eleven fighters and one bomber. Three more raids followed on the 22nd, and that night Allied assault infantry dug in in front of the line, in hidden positions. All was now ready for the Battle of El Alamein.

The Allies had available to them at this time 605 fighters, 254 light and medium bombers and 61 heavy bombers, together with a limited number of transport and liaison aircraft. Axis strength comprised 347 fighters, 72 dive-bombers and 171 medium bombers, but Allied rates of serviceability were far higher, giving a much greater ratio of superiority in numbers actually over the front than these figures indicate. Order of Battle of the RAF in North Africa was as follows:

Headquarters, R.A.F. Middle East

60 SAAF Squadron (Det.)	Maryland
162 Squadron	Lodestar, Wellington
2 PRU	Spitfire, Hurricane, Beaufighter
1411 Met. Flight	Gladiator

Air Headquarters Levant
1413 Met. Flight	Gladiator
1438 Flight	Blenheim

213 GROUP

241 Wing
451 Squadron	Hurricane

Western Desert Air Force
1 Air Ambulance Unit	DH 86

3 SAAF Wing
12 SAAF, 24 SAAF Squadrons	Boston
21 SAAF Squadron	Baltimore

232 Wing
55, 223 Squadrons	Baltimore

285 Wing
40 SAAF, 208 Squadrons	Hurricane, Tomahawk
60 SAAF Squadron	Baltimore
1437 Strategic Reconnaissance Flight	Baltimore
2 PRU (Det.)	As above

211 GROUP

6, 7 SAAF Squadrons	Hurricane 2D

233 Wing
2 SAAF, 4 SAAF, 260 Squadrons	Kittyhawk
5 SAAF Squadron	Tomahawk

239 Wing
3 RAAF, 112, 250, 450 Squadrons	Kittyhawk

244 Wing
92, 145, 601 Squadrons	Spitfire 5
73 Squadron	Hurricane

212 GROUP

7 SAAF Wing
80, 127, 274, 335 Squadrons	Hurricane

243 Wing
1 SAAF, 33, 213, 238 Squadrons	Hurricane

(Also attached to WDAF were US 12th Bombardment Group with B-25 Mitchells, and 57th Fighter Group with P-40F Warhawks; each Group comprised three squadrons, and was equivalent to an RAF Wing.)

Air Headquarters, Eygpt
250 Wing
89 Squadron	Beaufighter night-fighter

94 Squadron	Hurricane, Spitfire
252 Wing	
46 Squadron	Beaufighter night-fighter
417 Squadron	Hurricane, Spitfire

201 GROUP

15 SAAF Squadron	Bisley
47 Squadron	Beaufort
203 Squadron	Blenheim, Baltimore, Maryland
230 Squadron	Sunderland, Dornier Do 22 (ex Yugoslav Naval Air Force)
252, 272 Squadrons	Beaufighter strike fighter
459 Squadron	Hudson
1 General Reconnaissance Unit	Wellington
Sea Rescue Flight	Wellington, Fairchild
235 Wing	
13 (Hellenic) Squadron, 47 Squadron (Det.)	Blenheim
459 Squadron (Det.)	As above
247 Wing	
203 Squadron (Det.)	As above
221 Squadron (Det.)	Wellington
248 Wing	
38, 221, 458 Squadrons	Wellington
39 Squadron	Beaufort

205 GROUP

Special Liberator Flight	Liberator
231 Wing	
37, 70 Squadrons	Wellington
236 Wing	
108, 148 Squadrons	Wellington
238 Wing	
40, 104 Squadrons	Wellington
242 Wing	
147, 160 Squadrons	Liberators
245 Wing	
14 Squadron	Marauder
462 Squadron	Halifax

E

216 GROUP

117 Squadron	Hudson transport
173 Squadron	Various liaison types
216 Squadron	Bombay, Hudson, Lodestar transports
267 Squadron	Various transport types

(Also operating with AHQ, Egypt were five Fleet Air Arm units, four with 201 Group, and two American heavy bombardment Groups, the 1st Bomb Group (Provisional) with one squadron of B-17s and one of B-24s, and the 98th Bomb Group with four squadrons of B-24s, all operating under the control of 216 Group.)

Additionally, there was:

Air Headquarters, Iraq

214 GROUP

237 Squadron	Hurricanes

215 GROUP

244 Squadron	Blenheim, Vincent, Catalina

Air Headquarters, Malta

89 Squadron (Det.)	Beaufighter night-fighter
227 Squadron	Beaufighter strike-fighter
69 Squadron	Baltimore, Spitfire, Wellington
126, 185, 229, 249, 1435 Squadrons	Spitfire 5

(Two detachments of Fleet Air Arm torpedo-bomber squadrons were also operating from the island.)

This Order of Battle shows clearly the great increase in strength of the RAF in the Mediterranean since the start of 1942. As can be seen, the Spitfire squadrons, joined by 73 Squadron, had now been formed into a new wing, while 4 SAAF Squadron had been re-equipped with Kittyhawks; the gathering of the majority of Hurricane squadrons into a new group within WDAF was also noteworthy.

The night bomber organization, 205 Group, had also been somewhat strengthened; 108 and 148 Squadrons had both been re-formed in the Middle East during 1941, while 40 and 104 Squadrons had originally served on Malta, but had moved on to Egypt more recently. In 242 Wing, 147 Squadron was only a servicing unit, and was not engaged on operations; the Group had lost one Wellington unit when 38 Squadron transferred to 201 Group for Naval Co-operation duties, in which it was joined by two further similarly-equipped squadrons, 221 and 458. These undertook mine-laying and torpedo-dropping by night as their main duties. 13 (Hellenic) Squadron had been formed from Greek escapees, and was involved in general reconnaissance and anti-submarine patrols. The various liaison and communications units had in a couple of cases received aircraft of greater capacity and range, so that three transport squadrons were now available.

At 2140 hours on October 23rd 1942, the guns opened up in a barrage of a violence and weight unprecedented since the great battles of the Western Front twenty-five years earlier. After some intruder activity by Hurricanes of 73 Squadron and Beaufighters of 46 Squadron during the night, WDAF was in the air in force with the dawn, hammering the Axis at all points. The second day of the battle proved very busy in the air as attack after attack was made to break up enemy attempts to concentrate their forces, and many very fierce combats were fought. Beauforts and Bisleys, escorted by Beaufighters of 252 Squadron, successfully attacked a small, but vital convoy approaching Tobruk, while other Beaufighters of 272 Squadron intercepted 35 Ju 52s flying in precious fuel from Crete, and shot down four of them.

Despite the battering inflicted by both the artillery and the bombers on the Axis defences, it became clear that there would be no quick and easy breakthrough when an alarming toll of Allied armour was taken by a screen of anti-tank guns. On the 26th the Axis launched a counter-attack, but this was beaten off easily. In the air they threw in everthing they had, including Ju 87s and Italian CR 42 biplane fighters, used in the ground attack role, and many encounters took place, the Allied fighters once more suffering heavy losses while intercepting enemy formations and while escorting the frequent bombing raids. These continued to pound away at the mobile units of the Afrika Korps, again and again preventing them from forming up for further counter-attacks. Late on the 26th Beauforts of 47 Squadron, Bisleys of 15 SAAF Squadron and Beaufighters of both 252 and 272 Squadrons attacked a convoy making for Benghazi, sinking several ships. At dusk Wellington torpedo-bombers attacked, sinking the survivors – including a tanker carrying fuel for Rommel's tanks and aircraft – within sight of the port.

Montgomery decided on October 28th to abandon his original plan for a breakout in the north, but to keep up the pressure here to draw all Axis reserves to that area, and then strike in the centre, against the

Italian-held sector of the line; this new plan was codenamed 'Operation Supercharge'. During the last days of the month activity in the north remained violent, the Australian Infantry Division gaining a little ground, while German counter-attacks broke on a wall of steel. Overhead the battle in the air continued on its remorseless course; although still able to inflict grievous casualties, the Luftwaffe fighters could only marginally affect Allied operations, failing to stop the bombers and fighter-bombers attacking where and when they wished; Allied air superiority was now verging on supremacy.

Further attempts to supply Rommel by air proved expensive on October 30th, when Beaufighters and Kittyhawks shot down seven Ju 52s. On November 1st Kittyhawks of 112 Squadron, joined by US P-40s of the 66th Fighter Squadron, engaged 30 Ju 87s over the front, claiming seven shot down with seven more probables.

'Operation Supercharge' was put into effect on November 2nd, New Zealand infantry breaking through the Italian line to allow armour to pour through and roll up the Axis line to the north. Even now, however, the tanks found themselves once more held by the indefatigable anti-tank guns, and were unable to exploit the New Zealanders' success. However, it was clearly only a matter of time, and seeing the danger, Rommel decided that evening that he must withdraw if he was to prevent his army being routed. Again the Luftwaffe's Stukas were thrown in, but the Allied air force was everywhere, Hurricanes of 213 and 1 SAAF Squadrons claiming five and four probables.

The next day, while the RAF blasted the anti-tank screen holding up the Eighth Army's breakout, the Stukas again appeared over the front. One formation was met by Hurricanes of 33 and 238 Squadrons, and by Spitfires of 145 Squadron, which between them claimed three of the bombers and one of their escorts for the loss of two Spitfires. Later in the day more Hurricanes, this time from 80 and 127 Squadrons, intercepted twenty-five more Ju 87s, the former unit claiming seven, with nine more probably shot down. The German escorts were right on the ball this time, however, and savaged 127 Squadron which was flying top cover to 80, shooting down six of the Hurricanes; as a result of this attack, the squadron was unable to effectively engage the bombers and claimed only three probables. Throughout the 3rd Allied fighter losses were particularly severe.

At midday, however, reconnaissance aircraft spotted the first columns of enemy vehicles beginning the westward move down the coast road, and at once the pursuit was on, every available aircraft being directed to attack the tempting targets so offered. The following day the Eighth

Army finally made a general breakthrough, as, despite orders from Adolf Hitler to hold every foot of ground to the last, the Afrika Korps began to move back towards Libya in ever increasing numbers. All day medium and light bombers, fighters and fighter-bombers flew up and down the road at low level, bombing and strafing the close-packed and almost defenceless stream of lorries, cars, tanks and other vehicles that stretched nose to tail for mile after mile. The Axis fighters tried desperately to protect the columns, again inflicting substantial losses, but their efforts were to no avail.

Now becoming desperately short of fuel, the Luftwaffe was forced to evacuate the Fuka complex of landing grounds and move further back, and on November 5th after a short battle with the rearguards, the Allied spearheads had reached this area. Heavy rains on the 6th bogged down many Allied air units, and on the ground the pursuit was slow to get under way. Spitfires intercepted and shot down more Stukas on the 7th, and on this same day Kittyhawks shot down another four fuel-carrying Ju 52s approaching from Crete. The 8th, however, brought momentous news which was to change the whole face of the war in the Desert; the Allies had landed in French North Africa.

'Operation Torch'

Early November in Malta had again been very quiet, but on the 6th Beaufighters of 272 Squadron and Wellingtons of 104 Squadron from Egypt suddenly arrived; the reason for their presence was soon to become apparent. At this stage the defences of the island had claimed, since Italy's entry into the war, some 915 victories, 733 by the fighters and 182 by the guns. The defenders were not, however, to have to face another 'blitz' as the Anglo-American invasion of Algeria and Morocco, with the immediate threat that this posed to Tunisia, necessitated the deployment of all available aircraft from Sicily to this new front, thus effectively putting an end to any possibility of renewing the assault on the island.

The Allied landings, made at three widely-separated points under the general codename 'Operation Torch', were initially supported by carrier-borne aircraft of the US and Royal Navies, but squadrons of both the RAF and USAAF were ready to fly in in force the moment airfields were available, to take over from the naval air arms. The landings at Casablanca, on Morocco's Atlantic seaboard, and at Oran in Western Algeria, were to be predominantly American affairs, but that at Algiers, furthest east and nearest to Axis territories was mainly British, and it was to here that the RAF units involved would initially go.

A single ship had sailed with the main invasion fleets from England, but had put into Gibraltar a couple of days before the landings and disgorged the pilots of two American fighter groups and three British fighter wings, who at once set to work to assist in erecting and preparing their fighters, which had been delivered in crates in advance. The RAF units were:

322 Wing

81, 154, 242 Squadrons	Spitfire 5

323 Wing

43, 253 Squadrons	Hurricane 2C

324 Wing

72, 93, 111, 152 Squadrons	Spitfire 5
225 (Army Co-operation) Squadron	Hurricane 2C

Additionally 4 PRU with Spitfire 4s also arrived. Already on Gibraltar, and available to assist in initial operations, were another photographic reconnaissance Spitfire unit, 544 Squadron, and four general reconnaissance Hudson squadrons, 48, 233, 500 and 608, the two latter having only just arrived especially for 'Operation Torch'. Four squadrons of Bisley bombers, 13, 18, 114 and 614, comprising 326 Wing, were to fly out from England as soon as airfields were available, as were the Beaufighter night-fighters of 255 Squadron, unfortunately with their AI radar removed for security reasons.

The Vichy French put up a brief resistance to the Americans at Casablanca and Oran, but at Algiers little was met. As soon as the news that the troops had gone ashore reached Gibraltar, 43 Squadron's Hurricanes were launched, carrying only enough fuel for the one-way journey. Fortunately on arrival Maison Blanche airfield was found to be already in Allied hands, and the fighters were able to land safely. They were quickly joined by the Spitfires of 81 and 242 Squadrons, but conditions were initially chaotic, there being no food or shelter for the pilots, while supplies of fuel and ammunition were questionable to say the least.

In Sicily Generalfeldmarshal Kesselring, the ranking German officer, acted with considerable speed and decision, flying troops at once to Tunis, followed within hours by Bf 109s and Ju 87s. Reinforcements were poured across as quickly as the transports could off-load and fly back to collect them, and before the local French forces, dithering in a state of shock, could decide to whose side they should rally, Axis troops were firmly in control.

Every available bomber in Sicily was also readied to attack the Allied shipping and stores at Algiers, and during the evening of November 9th about 30 Ju 88s and He 111s swept in at low level. Beyond the range of fighter escort, the bombers were met by anti-aircraft fire and by the fighters of all three RAF squadrons, which mauled them terribly, claiming thirteen shot down. An indication of the weight of defence met is that not one of the bombers was to return undamaged to its base.

Eager to reach Tunis at the earliest opportunity to forestall just the

German reaction which was in fact taking place, the British pushed a small convoy, escorted by one carrier, up the coast to the little port of Bougie on the 10th, landing going ahead unopposed. Spitfires and Hurricanes of 242 and 43 Squadrons were dispatched to patrol over the port, and these claimed several more bombers which arrived to attack as the ships unloaded.

Malta was, of course, taking an active part in these operations, and 69 Squadron carried out many reconnaissances of the whole area. Reports brought back by its crews of Axis aircraft already in Tunisia led to nine Beaufighters from the newly arrived 272 Squadron being sent out to strafe Tunis' El Aouina airfield, where nine transports and a large glider were claimed strafed to destruction, with many others damaged.

From Bougie on the 11th British forces at once moved forward fast towards Tunis along the tortuous road through the coastal hills. In retaliation for the Allied landings, the Germans now moved into the Unoccupied Zone of France, while their bombers from Sicily and Sardinia rained more bombs on Bougie. At Maison Blanche the first Bisleys began arriving, joined by 111 Squadron which flew across from Gibraltar.

The next day Hurricanes escorted US C-47 transports to drop British paratroops on the airfield at Bone, well to the east of Bougie; their arrival just forestalled a similar move by the Germans, and 81 Squadron was able to fly up to this new forward base the moment it was secure. At the same time 154 Squadron came over from Gibraltar and moved to an airfield at Djidjelli, near Bougie, which had not yet been occupied; fuel was at once rushed forward by a small convoy of lorries, and at dusk the squadron was in the air to join 43 Squadron's Hurricanes from Algiers in repelling another raid on Bougie during which seven bombers were claimed shot down.

November 13th brought a series of heavy raids on Bougie and Djidjelli during which the defenders claimed six victories, and the first raids were also suffered at Bone, where 81 Squadron was joined by 111. The RAF was building up fast now, 93, 225 and 253 Squadrons flying in on this date, followed next day by 152 Squadron and 4 PRU. The Malta Beaufighters were extremely active, patrolling the area between Tunis and Sicily in an effort to intercept the streams of air transport now flying between these points. 227 Squadron was lucky in this respect on the 14th, claiming six shot down with several more probables.

Ths raids on Bone and Djidjelli were but a prelude to what was to come, as more Axis aircraft were rushed to airfields in Tunisia, experienced units from both Eastern and Western Fronts being withdrawn and rushed south to face the new threat. On November 16th 72 and 93 Squadrons moved to a new strip which had been hastily prepared at Souk el Arba, even nearer the Tunisian border than Bone, and the next day 225 Squadron moved to Bone to undertake tactical reconnaissance duties. On this latter date the Bisleys of 18 Squadron entered action, but lost four aircraft during the day – a sound indication that their equipment was not up to the job. From Egypt the night-flying Beaufighters of 46 Squadron flew over to Malta to begin night intruder activities over the Sicilian landing grounds.

On November 18th, 72 Squadron moved up to Bone leaving Maison Blanche where the congestion was now tremendous, as more and more Allied aircraft flew in. During the night of the 20th–21st Axis bombers delivered a sharp attack here, destroying a substantial number of British and American aircraft on the ground. Without their radar, the newly arrived Beaufighters of 255 Squadron were almost helpless, and to hold the fort while AI equipment was hastily flown out from England, six radar-equipped Beaufighters from 89 Squadron in Egypt were despatched on detachment, arriving at Algiers on the 24th.

With the opening up of Bone as the major British forward supply base, the importance of Bougie as a target dwindled, and raids here decreased, allowing 242 Squadron, which had joined 154 at Djidjelli, to move on to Bone. The army was now across the frontier and approaching Tunis and Bizerta, but as the Germans began appearing in strength, resistance stiffened and the advance slowed in the mountain passes of northern Tunisia. The arrival of the latest types of German fighters at good all-weather bases close to the front put the RAF at a disadvantage, and a growing number of hard battles with the Luftwaffe began. At the same time the weather was rapidly deteriorating into one of the worst winters experienced in North Africa for many years.

The Malta Beaufighters continued to enjoy many successes during the rest of November, and their tally of transport aircraft grew rapidly, including a giant six-engined Bv 222 flying-boat, shot down by Flg Off Coate of 272 Squadron. At night, too, things were improving for the Beaufighters, radar sets arriving on November 27th for 255 Squadron, and for 600 Squadron, a second night-fighter unit which had just flown in. That night 89 Squadron's detachment, almost as if to show just what could be done when the proper equipment was available, shot down five He 111s in the Algiers area. The 27th, however, saw a reversal for the Spitfires at the front when two of the five sweeps undertaken were badly 'bounced', several aircraft being lost. It also saw the scuttling of the French fleet at Toulon to prevent its takeover by the Germans.

There was considerable fighting on November 28th as Allied forces attempted to capture Djedeida airfield, and on the 29th paratroops were dropped at Depienne to assist in the fighting, but Axis resistance was too strong and by the end of the day the airfield was back in enemy hands. Without the necessary strength to advance further, and with lines of communication to Bone, 120 miles to the west, poor to say the least, the advance now came to a halt, virtually within sight of the Plain of Tunis.

In Egypt the Eighth Army, greatly heartened by news of 'Operation Torch', pressed on. A rearguard action by the Afrika Korps at Sidi Barrani was soon swept aside on November 9th, and two days later came the last big attempt by the Luftwaffe to slow Allied progress as the spearheads reached Halfaya – a last effort which was doomed to failure. Kittyhawks of 2 SAAF Squadron intercepted 15 Ju 87s over the front, but were at once attacked by the escort which shot down two of the South African fighters. To make this attack, however, they left their charges unprotected and the rest of the Kittyhawks were able to wade in and claim eight shot down and four probables. An indication that the latter indeed appear to have gone down was given shortly afterwards when American P-40s of the 57th Fighter Group caught just three Ju 87s landing at their base and shot them all down for the loss of one P-40. Other squadrons of Kittyhawks had success in catching more Ju 52s, and by the end of a very successful day at least eleven Ju 87s, six Ju 52s, five Bf 109s, a Ju 88 and a Fi 156 had been claimed for the loss of six Kittyhawks and one P-40, all combats having taken place over the Gambut and El Adem area.

By this time most targets were getting beyond the range of the airfields at Sidi Haneish, and squadrons began moving forward; however, due to the retreat of the Axis air units, and to their critical shortage of fuel, enemy aircraft began to be met much less frequently. WDAF kept up its attacks on the retreating columns of the Axis, still suffering the occasional sharp loss when the enemy did appear overhead.

On November 13th in an audacious move the thirty-six Hurricanes of 213 and 238 Squadrons, forming part of 243 Wing, moved to Landing Ground 125, deep in the Cyrenaican desert far behind enemy lines. From here they suddenly launched a series of strafing attacks on Axis columns and airfields normally well beyond the range of such depredations, the victims being completely baffled as to where their tormentors had appeared from. After two days of such attacks a column was seen approaching, and it was feared that the presence of the wing at the landing ground had been discovered. All aircraft were ordered into the air and attacked the column, virtually wiping it out, but it was decided that the wing must be evacuated before more troops were sent, and it returned to Allied territory the next day. In fact the presence of the wing had not been discovered; the column had been the Italian garrison of Siwa Oasis retreating to the north before they were cut off by the Allied advance.

A new series of operations began on November 17th as the advance neared Benghazi. Fighters were sent forward to the port to catch transport aircraft from Sicily, now engaged in evacuating key personnel from the area. Kittyhawks and P-40s undertook these operations largely, and on the first day 250 Squadron surprised He 111s and Ju 52s in the circuit, shooting down six of the former and one of the latter, also destroying two He 111s and two SM 81s on the ground.

The next day the massacre of transports continued; 3 RAAF Squadron arrived in the area first, shooting down one Ju 52 and strafing two He 111s on the ground. 233 Wing then arrived and caught a formation of 20 Ju 52s in the air, 2 and 4 SAAF Squadrons claiming eight shot down between them, while 260 Squadron strafed Berca airfield where six or seven aircraft were seen, and Magrun, where thirty to forty were observed. During the attack two transports took off and both were at once shot down. Later in the day 250 Squadron again appeared, strafing three He 111s, two Ju 52s and a Ca 311, the attack being completed by 3 RAAF Squadron which returned to strafe two Ju 52s and several other aircraft. In all ten transports were destroyed on the ground during the day, while in the air another Ju 52 was shot down by a Hurricane of 33 Squadron, to make the total claimed in flight twelve for the day. On the 19th British armour reached Benghazi, and the fighters then moved forward to Martuba.

The speed of the advance and the limited supplies of useable airfields available now led to the majority of the Hurricane squadrons being left behind on defensive duties as other units moved forward. Having neither the performance of the Spitfire nor the load-carrying capabilities of the Kittyhawk, the Hurricane was really well past its best. 1 SAAF Squadron had already converted to Spitfires at the start of November and now moved forward to join 92, 145 and 601 Squadrons in 244 Wing, the only Hurricane units to go with the advance at this stage being the night intruders of 73 Squadron (also a part of 244 Wing) and the tactical reconnaissance aircraft of 40 SAAF Squadron. 1 SAAF

Squadron had its first engagements with its new Spitfires on November 27th, but the pilots were still suffering from 'Hurricane-Complex', and flying defensively; consequently they lost one aircraft in a combat during the morning and two more in the afternoon, claiming in return two Bf 109s.

Late in November the Afrika Korps at last halted its retreat, taking up positions once more on the El Agheila line. Montgomery stopped the Eighth Army short of this line and began building-up for an assault on it. Most targets were now beyond the range of the Bostons, Baltimores and Mitchells, and there were as yet no airfields available for them nearer the front. This, together with the general absence of the Axis air forces, led to a period of comparative quiet, in the air as well as on the ground.

On the Tunisian front at the start of December a stalemate also existed, but it was far from being quiet. American long-range heavy day-bombers – B-17s mainly, had now arrived in Algeria, together with P-38 fighters to escort them, and they had begun a series of raids on Bizerta and Tunis. American troops had also now reached the front, taking up positions to the south of the British First Army, as the forces here had now become, the Americans being joined by French forces from Tunisia who had finally rallied to the Allied cause. The heaviest fighting at this time was still concentrated in the north, both on the ground and in the air.

Both of the RAF Spitfire wings were now in the forward area, 322 having set up at Bone, while 324 was at Souk el Arba. 323 Wing was responsible with its Hurricanes for the defence of the rear areas and of convoys along the coast, and was still based at Maison Blanche and Blida, joined by 241, 89, 255, 13 and 614 Squadrons. 18 Squadron's Bisleys and 600 Squadron's Beaufighters had joined 154 Squadron near Bougie, flying from Djidjelli and Canrobert airfields. New arrivals at Blida were the Wellingtons of 142 and 150 Squadrons, fresh from England.

The Axis had also been greatly reinforced, and were well situated to make life very unpleasant for the Allies. Initially Bone and Souk el Arba had no early warning radar and had to rely on spotters on near-by hills. Consequently, on the occasions when warning of a raid was received, it was seldom soon enough, and some hard battles were fought over these airfields. Apart from defensive sorties, the duties of the Spitfires centred around sweeps over the front, strafing sorties, and excorts to Bisleys, tactical reconnaissance aircraft, and Hurri-bombers.

The Germans launched their first counter-offensive on December 1st, involving the First Army in some desperate fighting to prevent being pushed back into Algeria. The Bisleys were thrown in to the attack, flying mission after mission under the watchful eyes of their Spitfire escorts. However, on the 4th came the call for yet another raid, but this time no escorts were available. A fighter sweep was in progress over the front at the time, so the risk was taken to let the bombers go alone. Ten Bisleys of 18 Squadron with two from 614 Squadron set out to attack a forward enemy airfield, seeing Spitfires of the sweep engaged in battle above as they approached. They were spotted early, however, and some sixty German fighters were waiting for them, attacking them on the way to and from, and over the target. Every bomber was shot down, including that of 18 Squadron's commanding officer, Wg Cdr H. G. Malcolm, who had pressed home his attack with great daring, and whose aircraft was one of the last to be shot down; Malcolm was awarded a posthumous Victoria Cross, the first to be awarded to an airman in the Mediterranean since the outbreak of war.

A new forward landing ground at Medjez el Bab was ready for use on December 5th and 93 Squadron moved forward to operate there in defence of the troops in the front line, who were now suffering regular attacks by Ju 87s. On arrival the Spitfires were 'bounced' by Fw 190s which were patrolling overhead as the British came in to land, and two Spitfires were shot down, the rest all being badly damaged and having to return to their base immediately. During the day 255 Squadron moved up to Souk el Arba and that night gained its first successes in Africa, two crews shooting down no less than five He 111s between them in the Bone area. Weather, however, was now abominable, and aircraft at the Bone and Souk el Arba airfields were frequently bogged in. More help was on the way as, on December 7th, a ship docked at Philippeville, bringing from England three more fighter squadrons, 32 (Hurricanes), 232 and 243 (Spitfires).

Probably the most successful operations at this time were those flown by the squadrons on Malta. The Beaufighters were now often joined by Spitfires on their patrols over the vital stretch of sea, and many a transport fell foul of them; they also strafed and sometimes bombed shipping in the area. A second Bv 222 flying-boat was shot down on December 10th, and on the 11th Beaufighters of 272 Squadron and Spitfires of 249 Squadron engaged a formation of 32 Ju 52s, escorted by twin-engined fighter types, claiming eight of the transports and five of the escort shot down.

By December 21st 241 Squadron had moved to Souk el Arba to

undertake the same mixture of tactical reconnaissance and close support work being carried out by 225 Squadron; 32 Squadron joined the other Hurricane units of 323 Wing in the rear. The next day a new British advance began and for several days all units at the front were engaged in some very hard fighting. The desperate need for good, all-weather airfields was eased on the 23rd when the first of a new complex on a well-drained site at Souk el Khemis was declared ready, 93 and 111 Squadrons moving in at once. On Christmas Eve the new offensive, designed to reach Tunis, was called off, defeated not by the enemy, but by the weather, which had turned even worse.

To the east in Libya activities in December remained rather quiet. Few units were close enough to the front to take an active part, and most sorties were flown by 239 and 244 Wings, the 57th Fighter Group, and the Beaufighters of 252 Squadron. With the decision to leave the Hurricanes behind, there had been a little revision of wing numbering. 233 Wing now took on the mantle of 7 SAAF Wing, and 260 Squadron moved over to join 239 Wing, so that the former was now for the first time a truly all South African unit. At the same time 5 SAAF Squadron began at last to dispose of its faithful Tomahawks – the last still on active duty anywhere in the world, and to replace them with Kittyhawks. In the Delta the Wellington squadrons of 236 Wing, 108 and 148, were both disbanded, the wing also ceasing to exist.

Over the front the main activity was fighter-bomber raids by the Kittyhawks and P-40s, 'de-loused' by the Spitfires. German fighters were beginning to appear regularly again, but in small numbers, and there were some short but sharp encounters. A rather more exciting attack was made on the 21st when six 3 RAAF Squadron Kittyhawks strafed the airfield at Hun. There were nine assorted aircraft and two gliders on the ground here, and seven were seen in flames as they left. Three days later the attack was repeated by 250 Squadron. The year ended on a particularly good note for 239 Wing when on December 30th 260 Squadron was able to 'bounce' six Bf 109s during the morning and to claim five of them shot down. In the afternoon 3 RAAF Squadron was equally fortunate, seven Kittyhawks engaging fifteen Bf 109s and shooting down three for no loss.

The New Year of 1943 thus found WDAF with only a relatively small part of its force in regular contact with the enemy. Apart from the units already mentioned, 2 PRU (Spitfires) and 1437 Strategic Reconnaissance Flight (Baltimores) were both flying regularly over enemy territory, as were the heavy bombers of 205 Group, still situated in the Delta. This striking force now included 37, 40, 70 and 104 Squadrons with Wellingtons, the last of these units recently returned from Malta, 462 Squadron with Halifaxes and 160 Squadron with Liberators; this latter unit would shortly be re-formed in the Far East, the remaining aircraft and personnel in Egypt together with various personnel of 147 and 159 Squadrons, forming a new squadron, 178. The other Wellington squadrons, 221 and 458, had moved from Berca to Malta for anti-shipping activities, leaving only 38 Squadron for these duties in the Eastern Mediterranean. The light bomber, transport and US bomber units remained unchanged, and the squadrons now left behind on defensive duties were 6, 33, 80, 127, 213, 238, 274, 335 and 7 SAAF Squadrons, the tactical reconnaissance units 208, 237 and 451 Squadrons also remaining in Egypt, Palestine and Iraq.

Of the night-fighters, 46 Squadron now had detachments at Edcu, Benghazi and on Malta, where 89 Squadron still also maintained a detachment, as well as in Algeria and Egypt. 14 Squadron had completed its conversion to Marauders during December and had moved forward into Libya to undertake shipping reconnaissance and torpedo-dropping operations.

Early in January Axis fighters became much more aggressive once more and a number of attacks were made by them on forward WDAF airfields. Several such attacks were made on Tamet on the 11th, a big Italian raid being intercepted by 92 Squadron, Flg Off N. F. Duke shooting down two MC 202s. The next day the Italians repeated the attack, and this time were intercepted by 145 Squadron which shot down a number of MC 200s.

The Eighth Army was now nearly ready to assault the Agheila/Buerat line, and on the 13th Allied air units really got their opening attack on these positions under way, the light bombers of 3 SAAF Wing now having moved up within range of the front. This first day was marked by the most aggressive counter-action by Axis fighters which, for the first time in many months, broke through to the bombers and shot down three Baltimores of 21 SAAF Squadron, six Kittyhawks and a P-40 also being lost. The next day Kittyhawks escorting Bostons were even harder hit, eleven being shot down against a claim for three attackers probably destroyed; this time, however, the bombers went unscathed.

On January 15th the Eighth Army opened its attack on the Buerat line, but before any real fighting had begun, Rommel withdrew his troops to a new line, Homs/Tarhuna. Here they fought only a rearguard action, and by the 19th Homs was in British hands; the advance was once more on, and WDAF began moving forward again. Tripoli was evacuated on January 22nd after heavy demolitions to the harbour had been carried out, and the Axis then began entering the defences of the Mareth Line, a strongly-fortified line just across the frontier into Southern Tunisia, originally built by the French in case of aggression from Mussolini's Libya. Here the Afrika Korps was to stand once more, and the Eighth Army again came to a halt to begin the build-up anew. The strength of the defences facing them were to prevent any move being made for some two months, while the port facilities of Tripoli were repaired to allow sufficient supplies to arrive.

In the north the New Year opened violently with heavy attacks on Bone harbour on January 1st by Ju 87s and escorting fighters. To strengthen the defences, an American Spitfire squadron, the 2nd, was loaned to the RAF, and was in action on January 2nd when a repeat attack was made. During one scramble the defenders were caught at a considerable disadvantage and six Spitfires were shot down, five of these being aircraft of 242 Squadron.

After these attacks, however, the month became quieter in the air – to a large extent due to the appalling weather conditions – but further raids on Bone were suffered. The completion of additional landing grounds in the Souk el Khemis area allowed reinforcement of the front, 154 Squadron moving up from Djidjelli. A third night-fighter squadron, 153, had now arrived from England, and this unit also moved its Beaufighters up to the Bone area. Nearly all raids by German and Italian medium and heavy bombers were now being made at night, and during the month a very heavy toll of these was taken by the Beaufighters. On the ground the stalemate on the First Army front continued, but there was more activity further south where the Americans struggled to consolidate their positions in the face of growing Axis pressure, culminating late in the month with a German attack on the US and French positions at Ousseitla; by January 30th the French had been driven off the Faid Pass and German forces were attacking the town of Pichon.

By January German night-fighters had arrived in Tunisia, and Wellingtons and Bisleys (now operating only at night) began to meet them quite frequently over Tunis and Bizerta, a number of bombers being lost. Early in February 18 and 114 Squadrons were ordered to hand in their Bisleys and await re-equipment with more modern types. On Malta the Beauforts of 39 Squadron had suffered heavy losses recently while operating by night, mainly in a mine-laying capacity, and late in January the squadron moved to Shallufa. January marked, however, the arrival on Malta of the first Mosquitos in the Mediterranean, night intruder Mark 2s of 23 Squadron, which arrived from England and at once began sorties over Sicily.

Perhaps the most important new arrivals at this time were the first Spitfire 9s, which were issued initially to 81 Squadron. The delighted pilots, after a short rest in Gibraltar while re-equipping, returned to the front at the end of January and on the last day of the month intercepted and shot down several Bf 109s without loss. 72 Squadron then withdrew to receive these aircraft, while the somewhat battered 242 Squadron was also taken out of the line for a badly-needed rest. The remaining night-fighter squadron at the rear, 600 Squadron, which was still in the Bougie area, moved forward to Souk el Khemis, the number of attacks being made on the former port and on Algiers now being negligible compared with the number of sorties by enemy bombers over the Bone area. At Maison Blanche 43 Squadron became the first unit of 323 Wing to begin conversion to Spitfire 5s.

Now safely behind the Mareth Line, Rommel took the opportunity while the Eighth Army was still unready to launch an attack on his forces, to attempt to clear his rear right flank, where the Americans were pressing into Southern Tunisia. Turning a part of his force of hardened veterans towards the north-east, he launched a lightning thrust against the inexperienced Americans and ill-equipped French on February 14th, quickly taking Sidi Bou Zid and advancing on the Kasserine Pass. The Allies were caught completely off balance and retreated in confusion. On the 17th units of the British First Army were rushed southwards to reinforce the French at Sbiba.

This damaging attack had one immediate benefit to the Allies; it put an end once and for all to the fragmented command structure, and led to the immediate appointment on February 18th of a combined and co-ordinated command at all levels. Admiral Sir Andrew Cunningham was appointed Commander in Chief Mediterranean, and General Alexander became Commander of Allied 18th Army Group, comprising First, and Eighth Armies, the US II Corps and the French XIX Corps. Alexander at once visited all fronts and was appalled by much that he found. He issued immediate orders that there was to be no Allied withdrawal beyond the Western Dorsale, the mountain barrier separating southern and central Tunisia from Algeria, and that no ground was to be given up at Sbiba and Kasserine.

Fortunately for the Allies there was at this time no overall Axis command in Africa; Rommel was desperately trying to persuade von Arnim, his opposite number in the north, to launch a combined offensive

F

from that area, and such a move might well have thrown the Allies back into Algeria. As it was, despite Alexander's order, the Americans were driven out of Kasserine, and Rommel's forces approached Thala. At this stage the British 6th Armoured Division was thrown into the struggle, at once becoming involved in heavy fighting. This new formation was able to hold its ground, and the Americans and French, after bitter fighting, were also now at last enabled to hold the line as more reinforcements were thrown in.

Alarmed by the speed with which the Allies were being reinforced, and dismayed by the failure of von Arnim to support his offensive, Rommel decided to withdraw from Sbiba and Kasserine on the 22nd in secret. By a quirk of fate a unified Axis command was set up the next day, just too late, and by the end of the month everything lost by the Americans had been regained.

During the Kasserine battle the RAF took little part; the area of the fighting was mainly the responsibility of the US XII Air Support Command, which suffered very heavy losses at this time, and British activity was largely limited to increased patrolling over the front by Spitfires in an effort to draw off some of the Luftwaffe units. With the move southwards of the 6th Armoured Division, a few sorties were made over the Kasserine area, particularly by the reconnaissance and close-support aircraft of 225 Squadron and their fighter escorts.

In the midst of the fighting, following the reorganization of the command structure, a complete reorganization of the Allied air forces was also undertaken. Air Chief Marshal Sir Arthur Tedder was appointed Mediterranean Air Commander, his headquarters assuming control of all units of the US 9th and 12th Air Forces (the Desert and Tunisia respectively), and the RAF's three commands – Eastern (Tunisia), Middle East (Desert), Malta and Gibraltar. Tedder was to have three subordinate commands, North-west African Air Force, under Major General Carl Spaatz, USAAF, Middle East Air Command, under Air Chief Marshal Sir Sholto Douglas, and Malta Air Command under Air Marshal Sir Keith Park.

The first of these was the one which would bear the main responsibility for the continued fighting in Africa. Throughout all commands wherever possible American commanders were given British deputies, and vice versa. This was to lead to a unique degree of Anglo–American co-operation in future activities, and to greatly augment the effectiveness of the operations undertaken.

North-West African Air Force was broken down as follows:

North-West African Strategic Air Force under Gen. J. Doolittle;

under his command were the B-17s of the US 12th Air Force, their P-38 escorts, and the two Wellington squadrons of the RAF at Blida.

North-West African Tactical Air Force under Air Marshal Sir Arthur Coningham, commander up to that time of WDAF. His command included what was now to be known simply as the Desert Air Force, under its new commander, Air Vice-Marshal Harry Broadhurst, 242 Group – the First Army fighters and fighter-bombers, under Air Commodore K. B. B. Cross, and the US XII Air Support Command, plus a new Tactical Bomber Force under Air Commodore L. F. Sinclair, of which more later, and a Night Fighter Force under Gp Capt David Atcherley.

The final component of NWAfAF was North-West African Coastal Air Force, comprising 323, 325 and 328 Wings, RAF, 1st and 2nd Air Defence Wings, USAAF, and the US 350th Fighter Group, all under the command of Air Vice-Marshal Sir Hugh Pugh Lloyd.

Coningham's first action as commander of the new tactical air force was to order 242 Group and XII ASC to cease flying the defensively-orientated operations they had been mainly undertaking, and to start flying offensive patrols of the type practised for many months by WDAF. To assist in these, 242 Group was reinforced by the arrival back at Souk el Khemis of 72 Squadron with its new Spitfire 9s. The squadron arrived in heavy rain, which cut visibility, and in consequence five of the new fighters crash-landed, while a sixth was totally destroyed in a crash.

Just too late to coincide with Rommel's now-defunct offensive, the Axis armies in the north launched 'Operation Ochsenkopf' in the Sidi Nsir area on February 26th, First Army units at once becoming involved in a fierce battle. The RAF was thrown in to support the troops, Hurri-bombers of 241 Squadron, heavily escorted by Spitfires, being much in evidence. The new offensive was to be short-lived, however – meeting strong British resistance, it made little progress and it was in any event too late. The focus of attention was about to shift to the south.

The very day the new offensive began, Desert Air Force squadrons started their softening-up operations prior to the Eighth Army's forthcoming attack on the Mareth Line. Fighter-bombers were over the Mareth area all day, Spitfires providing top cover, but it was an inauspicious start, as Axis fighters were very active and no less than fourteen Kittyhawks were lost with others damaged.

There had been minor changes in dispositions during the weeks immediately preceding these activities; the Wellingtons of 37, 40, 70 and 104 Squadrons had moved up to Gardabia to throw the weight of their night attacks against Mareth, and the Canadian 417 Squadron, now re-equipped with Spitfires, had moved up to Tripoli to join 244 Wing. 46 Squadron had withdrawn to Edcu, but here 603 Squadron was reforming with Beaufighters as a day strike unit. 60 SAAF Squadron, whose long range reconnaissance activities had been much reduced recently by various troubles with its few Baltimores, now received (at Montgomery's personal request) a pair of photo-reconnaissance Mosquitos, and more would follow later. Tripoli was opened for the unloading of supplies on February 4th, and on the 22nd the first Eighth Army units crossed the Tunisian frontier. The DAF moving up and building up for the offensive generally, was again joined by 6 Squadron, once more ready to operate its Hurricane 2Ds against enemy armour.

After the opening days of the new air offensive, February 28th and March 1st were rather quiet, but during the evening of the latter day Axis artillery began shelling the forward landing ground at Hazbub Main where 244 Wing had just set up camp, and the squadrons were forced to retreat in a great hurry to Ben Gardane. In an effort to forestall Montgomery's impending attack, Rommel now launched an offensive of his own, sending the Afrika Korps down the Mareth–Medenine road on March 16th in an effort to catch the Eighth Army off balance. The attempt failed dismally; Montgomery used Rommel's own tactics, allowing the German armour to run up against a screen of anti-tank guns, and by midday the advance had come to an abrupt halt. The Afrika Korps began to retreat, leaving behind fifty-two tanks which it could ill-afford to lose. Poor weather prevented much participation by the air forces, but some Ju 87s did appear, one being shot down by 1 SAAF Squadron. It was to be Rommel's last offensive in Africa, and immediately afterwards, sick and dispirited, he left for Europe. His place in command of the Afrika Korps and units of the Italian army was taken by the Italian General Giovanni Messe, and the force was retitled First Italian Army. The post of supreme commander in Tunisia, which many had thought Rommel would fill, now went to von Arnim.

Far away in the Southern Sahara, in the French territory of Chad, Free French forces under General LeClerc had been ready to join in the main fighting for a long time. Now the opportunity at last offered itself to join up with Allied forces, and LeClerc's men made the long and arduous journey across the Sahara, finally approaching Ksar Rhilane in south-west Tunisia, where it was planned they would link up with the Eighth Army's left flank and fill part of the gap still existing between this and the right flank of US II Corps. As they neared their objective on March 10th von Arnim dispatched a strong column to attack them, but DAF was thrown into their support, launching a series of strong fighter-bomber attacks. 6 Squadron's 'tank-busters' made an effective return to action, claiming twelve of twenty vehicles they attacked in one mission, put out of action. The Luftwaffe was quick to spring to the defence of the hard-pressed column, however, and as one Kittybomber attack went in, 112 Squadron, which was providing top cover, was hard hit by the Messerschmitts. While claims were made for three German fighters which raised the squadron's tally to over 200, six Kittyhawks were lost. The threat to the French was, however, neutralized, and they were able to take their place in the line.

The next day the New Zealand Division moved up to Ben Gardane in secret, ready for the new offensive, while all remaining units of DAF which were to take part, moved to their bases near the front. At last for the first time since the Alamein battle, both light bomber wings were back at the front. A most unusual reinforcement arrived on March 12th for 244 Wing in the shape of the Polish Fighting Team; commanded by Wg Cdr T. Rolski and led in the air by Sqn Ldr S. F. Skalski, this unique organization was composed entirely of combat-experienced, and specially selected volunteer pilots, and was attached for operations to 145 Squadron. It was to prove a most valuable addition to DAF strength.

On March 17th US II Corps moved forwards from the west, taking Gafsa in an abortive attempt to reach the Tunisian coast and cut off the forces in the Mareth Line from those in the north. During the night of the 19–20th the New Zealanders at Ben Gardane moved forward, swung far to the south to by-pass the Axis right flank and make for the Tebaga Gap in a classic outflanking advance. Twenty-four hours later as dusk fell the Eighth Army's main assault on the Mareth line began, but over difficult terrain and in the face of strong defences, progress was extremely slow and hard. The main activities of the fighter-bombers and 'tank busters' of DAF was in support of the New Zealanders, now meeting tanks rushed from Mareth to intercept them.

Activity in this area continued on the 22nd, and Hurricane 2Ds of 6 Squadron claimed nine tanks south of El Hamma on an early sortie, losing three of their aircraft in return; later in the day a fourth was shot down. That night Montgomery decided that he had probably drawn all the Axis reserves to Mareth by his frontal attack, and now switched his main attack to the Tebaga Gap. It was intended that for the first time DAF fighter-bombers would take an active part in the main battle, instead of striking at supplies and concentrations, and would operate immediately in front of the advancing troops. In order to draw away Axis fighters which could well inflict substantial losses during such operations, 242 Group and XII ASC were ordered to go flat out for air superiority over central and northern Tunisia.

To increase the effectiveness of the fighter cover afforded to the Kittyhawks and Hurricane 2Ds, a dozen Spitfire 9s were issued to 244 Wing on March 23rd, six going to 145 Squadron where they were to be used principally by the Poles, and four to 92 Squadron, the others being held in reserve. 242 Group dispatched the Hurribombers of 241 Squadron to Thelepte on the American front, from where they could assist the DAF fighter-bombers in the El Hamma area. During the day the Eighth Army bridgehead across the Wadi Zigzaou in front of the Mareth defences was quietly withdrawn, and every available unit was sent racing around the foot of the Matmata Hills after the New Zealanders.

Throughout the 24th DAF continued a series of massive attacks on the forces facing the New Zealanders, who had come to a halt before the Tebaga Gap, where the Axis had thrown up some formidable defences. These attacks continued on the 25th, but ground fire was very heavy and opposing fighters were appearing more often. 6 Squadron lost six of ten Hurricanes sent out, but by amazing good luck not a single pilot was hurt.

The great attack was made next day; fighter-bombers, now joined by Baltimores, Bostons and B-25s, attacked the enemy gun positions and strong points all day. Towards evening the artillery put down a heavy barrage, and some eighteen squadrons of fighter-bombers poured in at 1530 hours to saturate the defences. Half an hour later a second wave attacked as the troops began their advance, this wave suffering very heavy losses to flak, particularly some of the American units which were taking part. The attack was entirely successful, however, the aircraft keeping down the heads of the Axis gun crews, allowing the infantry to overrun them and the armour to pour through the gap with minimal losses.

The next day, to avoid being outflanked, the Axis forces on the Mareth Line were withdrawn, those units facing the great exodus of Allied armour from the Tebaga Gap just managing to hold the British tanks off long enough for their comrades to escape northwards, DAF units kept up the attack, both over the front and on the columns now fleeing north, but losses to both flak and fighters were heavy. Such German aircraft types as Fw 190s, Me 210s and Hs 129s were now being met in the south for the first time, and on March 28th Spitfires of 244

Wing caught a rare formation of Ju 88s over the front, shooting down three, two of which fell to the Poles. During the day the New Zealanders captured the town of Gabes, but the enemy forces reached a new defensive line at Wadi Akarit.

SAAF Kittyhawks caught a considerable number of MC 202 fighters on the ground at Achichina on the 29th, destroying five and damaging another twelve, but there were still plenty of Axis fighters around, and frequent engagements were fought. The Eighth Army's advance now brought DAF units very close to the area in which XII ASC operated, and to an increasing extent operations of the two air forces were to be intermingled. With the successful conclusion of the Mareth battle, 241 Squadron left Thelepte and returned north to Souk el Khemis.

With all Axis forces now in Tunisia, the sea route between here and Sicily became even more vital to the Axis, and in consequence shipping a more and more priority target for Allied air attacks. Ideally situated, the units on Malta initially predominated in this role; at night Mosquitos and Beaufighters from the island continued to intrude over Sicily, and also began to take an increasing toll of aircraft along the African coast. By day, attacks on shipping increased steadily, sometimes resulting in combats with escorting fighters, as on March 17th when a mixed force of Beauforts and Beaufighters ran foul of escorting Bf 110s and lost several of their number. Late in March the island received its first Spitfire 9s, a handful of these going to one flight of 126 Squadron.

In northern Tunisia both fighter wings were active, 72 Squadron adding to its sweeps a number of escort missions to American B-17s over Tunis and Bizerta. 152 Squadron was at this time issued with bomb racks, and became the first official Spitbomber squadron (as opposed to the unofficial bomb-carrying activities of 126 Squadron during the previous autumn). Despite the static nature of the front, there were regular combats over the area, particularly late in March as the Spitfires increased activities in support of the Eighth Army's Mareth operations.

On March 25th the new Tactical Bomber Force at last came into being. It comprised initially 326 Wing, two US groups and some French bomber units. 326 Wing, however, had only 13 and 614 Squadrons operational at this time. 18 and 114 Squadrons had been re-issued with Bisleys in February during the Kasserine battle, but had now again discarded these. 18 Squadron was at last receiving a few Bostons. Some of these came from 2 Group of Bomber Command in the United Kingdom, while others were in fact A-20 Havocs, borrowed from the US 47th Bomb Group.

In Algeria 323 Wing's duties were relatively un-exciting, but an opportunity for some real action came on March 27th when Axis bombers were sent out to attack a big convoy which was just arriving, and six of the attackers were shot down by the Spitfires and Hurricanes of 43 and 87 Squadrons.

By the end of the month a complete renumbering of the Photographic Reconnaissance Units had been completed; 2 PRU in Desert Air Force became 680 Squadron, while 4 PRU with 242 Group became 682 Squadron. On Malta 69 Squadron had for some months been operating one flight of photographic Spitfires, and this flight was now removed from the parent unit and formed into 683 Squadron. On the tactical reconnaissance side, DAF's 40 SAAF Squadron had now fully converted to Spitfire 5s, while in 242 Group 225 Squadron had also acquired a few of these aircraft for reconnaissance purposes.

The Final Assault

The regular and costly Allied attacks both in the air and by submarine and surface vessels, on shipping between Sicily and Tunisia were making it increasingly difficult to supply the large Axis forces in Africa adequately, and early in April an attempt was made to greatly increase the flow of vital items – particularly fuel – by air transport. Every possible transport aircraft was flown down to Sicily, and vast formations, escorted by all available fighters, began the short but dangerous journey from Europe to the Cap Bon peninsular, the closest landfall in Tunisia.

On April 5th the Allies launched 'Operation Flax', a series of patrols in strength designed to try and intercept these aircraft. Initially these operations were flown mainly by American P-38 Lightnings, the longest-ranging fighters available, but later in the month the approach of the Eighth Army within range of Cap Bon allowed DAF Kittyhawks and P-40s to join in.

In the north meanwhile, 242 Group kept up attacks on Axis airfields and flew sweeps over the front, while on April 6th the Eighth Army attacked the Wadi Akarit line and swiftly overwhelmed the Italian defenders. German forces then launched a counter-attack, but this was beaten off and the First Italian Army again retreated northwards. The next day the Eighth Army reached Mezzouna, and the First Army then opened a new offensive designed to join up with the spearheads from the south. Such a meeting was getting daily closer, and during April 7th the Eighth Army patrols met the first patrols from US II Corps near Gafsa. 6 Squadron was again to the fore in supporting the Desert veterans, but lost three Hurricanes on the 6th and six more on the 7th, virtually all to the ever-increasing flak. As a result of recent losses it was then regretfully necessary to withdraw the unit to re-equip.

As the First Army's offensive got under way the Luftwaffe once again threw in the Stukas, and during the 7th 243 Squadron intercepted fifteen of these, claiming five shot down and five probables. The advance met determined resistance, however, and on the 9th heavy tank losses were suffered at Djebel Rohrab. By dint of great effort, however, the 6th Armoured Division broke through the Fondouk Pass on the 10th and made for Kairouan, where contact was made with the Eighth Army, advancing from Sfax. The Axis were now being pressed into an ever-decreasing area of northern Tunisia, and were faced by a strong and united front from coast to coast.

Allied air power had increased vastly, and although the Axis, with their shorter lines of communication, were able to pump more fighters into Africa, these were unable, despite the toll they continued to take, to have any real effect whatsoever on Allied operations. To add to this, the Spitfire 9s, now appearing in growing numbers, were very much getting the upper hand over any Axis types they met; the number of Spitfires available generally was constantly increasing. From Tripoli, where it had been left on defensive duties, 417 Squadron now rejoined 244 Wing to give DAF five Squadrons of Spitfires, while to the west two of 323 Wing's other squadrons, 32 and 87, were also augmenting their Hurricanes with some of these fighters.

The Eighth Army and US II Corps had now fully converged, and on April 12th the Eighth entered Sousse, moving on next day to the foot of the Enfidaville Hills, where the Axis were again digging in. The relatively small area of Tunisia still in Axis hands was now literally deluged with bombs from an armada of bombers which flew over virtually unchallenged day and night. The light and medium squadrons of Bostons, Baltimores, Bisleys, A-20s, B-25s and B-26s were joined from east and west by B-17s, B-24s, Wellingtons, Halifaxes and Liberators. More and more of the many bombers could now be spared to direct their attacks on the supply ports and airfields in Sicily and Southern Italy, while B-25s and B-26s joined the fighter-bombers and Beaufighters in seeking out and destroying the shipping still trying to reach the now beleagurered forces in Africa. Axis bombers still tried to disrupt Allied convoys along the north coast, achieving the odd success, but generally they were driven off as on April 13th when Beaufighters of 255 Squadron were scrambled in daylight and intercepted bombers attacking one such convoy south of Sardinia, shooting down two.

DAF units were moving up to the north for a planned final assault at Enfidaville, and on April 16th Spitfires of 244 Wing on a sweep over Cap Bon spotted eighteen SM 82 transports. Diving to attack, they claimed seven of these aircraft, together with some Bf 109s of the escort which attacked them and shot down two of the Spitfires; the latter were flown by the wing leader, Wg Cdr I. R. Gleed, a most notable fighter pilot, who was killed, and his wingman, who managed to bale out.

By now the P-38s and Beaufighters had exacted a savage toll of the transport aircraft during their 'Operation Flax' patrols, but the true climax went to Desert Air Force. On April 18th Spitfires of 92 Squadron covered four squadrons of US P-40s over the Cap Bon area on a 'Flax' mission. Just before the patrol ended a huge formation of Ju 52s was seen leaving Tunisia just as the sun began to set. The Spitfires were only able to claim a few of the escorting fighters, but the Americans waded in with a vengeance, final claims being confirmed as fifty-nine transports and sixteen escorting fighters shot down.

On the next day the South Africans had their turn, when 7 SAAF Wing Kittyhawks engaged about eighteen more transports and their escort, claiming fifteen and four probables. A pair of Spitfires from 229 Squadron on Malta spotted twenty Ju 52s – possibly those later attacked by the South Africans, and shot down two stragglers.

During the night of April 19–20th the Eighth Army attacked the Enfidaville positions, confidently expecting to break through and sweep on into Tunis. They were to be disappointed, however, their Desert experience proving of no help to them in the steep and mountainous country into which they now tried to advance, country admirably suited to defence; strong resistance was met, and little progress could be made. Regretfully, Montgomery had to agree that the First Army should make the final push.

Preparations were going ahead for this, and 242 Group Headquarters had now moved forward to Thibau. Nearly all the Group's squadrons were now based at Souk el Khemis where seven good landing grounds, all named after London railway stations, were now in use. 18 Squadron had been joined by 114 Squadron, also re-equipped with Bostons, and both units resumed operational flying. 682 and 683 PR Squadrons had both received a few of the latest Spitfire 11s to supplement their ageing Mark 4s, and 225 Squadron had finally exchanged its last Hurricanes for Spitfire 5s, also borrowing a few newly arrived P-51A Mustangs from the USAAF for longer-range tactical work. 14 Squadron had moved its Marauders from Libya to northern Tunisia to join fully in the anti-shipping work around Cap Bon.

The main First Army offensive opened on April 22nd, and was heralded by a final great slaughter of transports when 7 SAAF Wing, joined by 1 SAAF Squadron and some units of 239 Wing, engaged twenty Me 323s, enormous six-engined transports, which were cut to pieces. Claims in total were a little optimistic, including twenty-five (!) Me 323s and ten escorting fighters for the loss of ten Kittyhawks and one Spitfire; actual loss of Me 323s was sixteen. The toll was too great, however, and the daylight formations of transports ceased, aircraft having to get across as best they could during the hours of darkness.

The Malta squadrons could still catch them, however, and in the early hours of April 28th Sqn Ldr J. J. Lynch of 249 Squadron shot down one Ju 52 and shared a second with his wingman, these being the 1000th and 1001st aircraft claimed by Malta's defences during the war. That same day in Tunisia von Arnim launched all his remaining armour in a counter-attack, retaking Djebel Bou Aoukaz; all elements of the air forces were at once thrown into the attack as the army strove to halt this final desperate fling. It was held on the 30th by the First Army, which inflicted heavy losses, leaving the Axis with only some sixty-nine tanks in Africa. Montgomery was now ordered to transfer some of his best units, 7th Armoured Division, 4th Indian Division and 201st Guards Brigade, to reinforce the First Army. This difficult move at the height of the battle was successfully and secretly accomplished, the units passing right across the rear of the French XIX Corps front to reach their new positions.

In the air Kittyhawks and P-40s still patrolled over Cap Bon, now after shipping which they successfully dive-bombed, but even at this late stage small numbers of determined Axis fighters were still frequently met. The use of increasing numbers of transport aircraft at night offered new opportunities to the night-fighter crews, and during the first grey pre-dawn of May 1st Flt Sgt A. B. Downing of 600 Squadron, assisted by his radar operator, Sgt Lyons, accomplished the outstanding feat of shooting down five Ju 52s in flames, one after the other in quick succession.

On the ground the first big breakthrough came on May 3rd when US 1st Armoured Division got through to Mateur. Three days later the First Army made a direct assault on Tunis, its own and the borrowed Eighth Army armoured divisions, well-supported from the air, taking Massicault and pressing on with great success next day. The 7th Armoured Division was first into the capital during the afternoon of the 7th, the Americans entering Bizerta only minutes later. Passing straight through, 7th Armoured turned right to seal off the larger part of the remaining Axis forces on the Cap Bon peninsula, while the 6th Armoured Division swung left to meet the Americans advancing from Bizerta.

Air support continued unabated, but there were now only tactical targets left. To avoid heavy losses on the ground, more and more of the remaining Axis fighter units were forced to retreat to Sicily, and to fly over each day to operate from the remaining landing grounds. Allied fighters strafed these landing grounds regularly, while fighter-bombers went after the disorganized forces packed into the Cap Bon area, hitting them continually. With so many troops concentrated into such a small area, the volume of ground fire was intense, and losses to this cause rose steeply during the final week of the campaign. Leaving Cap Bon to the fighter-bombers, the mediums now turned most of their attention to the islands of Pantelleria and Lampedusa, and to the airfields of Sardinia.

There were still odd groups of Axis fighters to be met, and on May 8th 93 Squadron caught twenty Bf 109s and a Ju 52 on the ground at Menzel Temime and strafed them thoroughly, followed by the Spit-bombers of 152 Squadron, which were rapidly directed to the scene. It was on this day that the final evacuation of Africa by the Axis air forces was made, and thereafter all sorties had to be flown from Sicily or Sardinia.

Increasing numbers of units were now able to direct their attentions elsewhere, and Malta-based Spitfires were quickly found to be well-placed to escort American heavy bombers over Sicily as the focus of attention began to swing to this area. Beaufighters of 252 and 603 Squadrons began a series of sweeps over the Ionian and Aegean Seas, after communication and transport aircraft; only by night did the Axis now venture over Africa, where several raids on the northern coastal area were launched, and were met by night-fighters which shot down several raiders. On May 11th fifteen Ju 88s approached at dusk, but Beaufighters of 153 Squadron intercepted and shot down two.

Two days later on May 13th, 1943, the last Axis forces on Cap Bon surrendered and all fighting ceased. During the final week 248,000 prisoners were taken, including fifteen German and seven Italian generals. Only 638 troops escaped to Europe, most by air, as a direct result of Allied air power, which was now supreme.

The Allied air forces had played a most important part in winning a great victory. In May 1943 they flew unchallenged and victorious above the whole Mediterranean coastline of Africa to which the Axis would not return. Now they prepared for an even greater venture – the Allied invasion of Southern Europe.

Acknowledgments

AVM J. H. Lapsley, Plates 1, 5, 6, 8, 12, 13, 15, 17, 18, 20, 25, 27.
E. C. R. Baker, Plate 42.
D. Becker via M. Schoeman, Plates 150, 154.
S. W. Donaldson via D. Becker/R. C. Jones, Plates 55, 56, 57.
Wg Cdr C. H. Dyson via E. C. R. Baker, Plate 26.
F. J. Henderson via R. C. Jones, Plates 107, 108, 116.
Imperial War Museum, Plates 9, 10, 11, 19, 21, 22, 23, 24, 28, 29, 30,
31, 32, 33, 35, 36, 37, 38, 39, 40, 41, 43, 44, 45, 46, 47, 48, 50, 51, 52,
54, 58, 59, 60, 61, 70, 71, 72, 73, 74, 75, 76, 77, 79, 80, 81, 82, 83, 84,
85, 86, 87, 88, 90, 91, 92, 93, 94, 95, 96, 97, 98, 99, 101, 102, 103,
104, 105, 106, 109, 114, 115, 118, 119, 120, 121, 122, 123, 124, 125,
126, 129, 131, 132, 134, 137, 138, 140, 141, 142, 143, 145, 147, 151,
153, 155, 156, 157, 158, 159, 160, 161, 162, 164, 165, 166, 167, 168,
169, 170, 171, 172, 173, 174, 175, 176, 178, 179, 180, 182, 183, 184,
185, 186, 187, 188, 189, 190, 191, 192, 193, 194, 195, 196, 197.
R. C. Jones, Plates 49, 53.
Via R. C. Jones, Plates 66, 67, 68, 69, 78, 117, 152, 168, 177.
M. Kester via N. Franks, Plates 2, 3, 4, 7, 16.
Newton via R. L. Ward/R. C. Jones, Plate 34.
I. Primmer, Plate 135.
RCAF, Plate 181.
H. Ring, Plate 89.
SAAF Official via K. Smy, Plates 100, 111, 113, 128, 133, 146, 148.
Wg Cdr Sheehan, Plate 144.
K. Smy, Plates 110, 112, 130.
Tandy, via R. C. Jones, Plate 139.
B. H. Vickery via R. C. Jones, Plate 149.
Gp Capt G. H. Westlake, Plates 62, 63, 64, 65, 127.

1 At the outbreak of the war in Europe, 80 Squadron was based at Amriya in Egypt. Flg Off J. H. Lapsley pilots Gladiator K7914 over the area shortly before camouflage paint was applied to all the squadron's aircraft.

2 Sgt Hulbert stands K7903 on its nose while landing; this was the aircraft normally flown by 'A' Flight commander, Flt Lt E. G. Jones.

3 Camouflage paint and squadron codes have been hurriedly applied to this 80 Squadron Gladiator, almost obscuring the fuselage roundel; the unit badge on the fin has been repainted. A.C. M. Kester lunches off the tailplane.

4 'B' Flight of 80 Squadron at Amriya, early 1940; cowlings, cockpits and wheels are shrouded against the intrusion of the ever-present, and highly-abrasive desert sand.

5 Just before the Italian entry into the war on June 10th 1940, the unit code letters of 80 Squadron were altered from GK to YK — probably to avoid confusion with 112 Squadron's GA. Re-lettered, and with the badge now removed from the fin, six of the squadron's Gladiator 1s are prepared for take off during the early days of the war.

6 Trailing a thick plume of dust, 'S' of 80 Squadron begins its take off run.

7 .... and off she goes. An 80 Squadron Gladiator gets airborne from Amriya.

8 An 80 Squadron Gladiator banks sharply to show how the port underside of the lower wing and fuselage have been painted black — standard R.A.F. fighter recognition 'camouflage' of the period. Note that the upper wing has not been similarly treated.

9 A trio of Westland Lysanders of 208 Army Co-Operation Squadron enter a turn as they cross the Suez Canal. One squadron of these aircraft was immediately available in Egypt in June 1940.

10 Although receiving Blenheim 4 'long-noses' at the start of the war in the Mediterranean, 113 Squadron still had short-nosed Mark 1s on hand when this photograph was taken a little earlier in 1940.

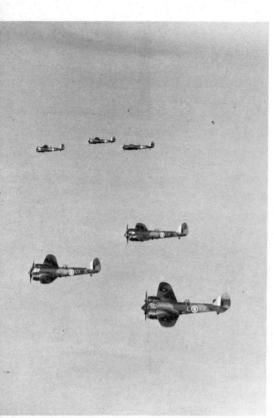

11 Blenheim 1s of 113 Squadron, their paintwork immaculate, fly a 'vic of vics' formation over the featureless surface of the Egyptian desert.

12 A young pilot of 80 Squadron who was soon to make a name for himself, Flg Off J. H. Lapsley, sits on a wheel of his Gladiator; note the local 'mod' to protect the oil cooler inlet from dust while not in flight.

13 Returning from a night flight, Flg Off G. T. Baynham crashed K7973 and badly damaged it; fortunately he was unhurt.

14 First Italian aircraft shot down in Africa fell to Flg Off V. C. Woodward of 33 Squadron on June 14th 1940; Woodward, a Canadian, was destined to be one of the top-scoring R.A.F. fighter pilots in the Mediterranean area. He is seen here in the cockpit of his Gladiator.

15 YK-O, L8011, was the aircraft of Flt Lt M. T. St. J. Pattle, flight commander of 'B' Flight, 80 Squadron. Pattle, who was probably the top-scoring R.A.F. fighter pilot of the whole war, was shot down in this aircraft during a fight with a large number of Italian CR 32s and CR 42s on August 4th 1940.

16 Also shot down on August 4th 1940 was L8009, YK-I, the aircraft of Flg Off P. G. Wykeham-Barnes. Engaged in escorting a Lysander of 208 Squadron over Bir Taib el Esem, three of four 80 Squadron Gladiators were shot down, Pattle and Wykeham-Barnes baling out and returning on foot; the third pilot was killed.

17 Flt Lt Pattle in flight in L8011.

18 80 Squadron in 1940 was a most outstanding unit. Apart from Pattle, several other pilots were to achieve distinction, and three of them were to become officers of Air rank, all three also shooting down substantial numbers of enemy aircraft. These three were, l. to r., Flg Off J. H. Lapsley, Flg Off P. G. Wykeham-Barnes and Sqn Ldr P. H. Dunn. In the background is one of the first Hurricanes to be received by the squadron.

19 All the Hurricanes initially delivered to Egypt in the summer of 1940 were delivered to 80 Squadron, being concentrated into 'C' Flight for the defence of Alexandria. Flying one of these aircraft Flg Off Lapsley, seen here in the cockpit of his Hurricane, had the first conclusive combat with the fast Savoia SM 79 bombers of the Regia Aeronautica when he shot down three on August 17th 1940.

20 One of the three Savoia SM 79s shot down by Flg Off Lapsley of 80 Squadron over Alexandria on August 17th 1940, crash-landed, and is here seen on display in the town.

21 On August 8th 1940, 80 Squadron Gladiators avenged the defeat suffered by them four days earlier. Going on patrol in much greater strength than before, 14 Gladiators engaged a formation of CR 42s and claimed 9 shot down with six more probables. Plt Off S. Linnard claimed two of the former; he is seen here in his Gladiator, showing his distinctive personal insignia on the fuselage.

22 By late 1940 sufficient Hurricanes had arrived for two full squadrons to be equipped. 274 Squadron was formed from 33 and 80 Squadron's 'C' Flights, while 33 Squadron was itself re-equipped. Here two Hurricanes of the latter unit come in to land at a forward airfield near Sidi Barrani, while a third is serviced.

23 A patrol of Hurricanes of 33 Squadron over the desert in line abreast formation. This squadron took a heavy toll of the Regia Aeronautica during the first month of the First Libyan Campaign, December 1940.

24 A Hurricane 1 test-fires its eight Browning machine guns into a small, but solidly-built stone butt in Egypt.

25 Flg Off V. C. Woodward of 33 Squadron puts on his parachute before climbing into his Hurricane in December 1940. Woodward was to claim five CR 42s in twenty days during the month. It is noteworthy that even at this early date, his Hurricane appears to be painted in the Desert camouflage scheme of brown and stone, later applied generally to all R.A.F. aircraft in Egypt from about the middle of 1941.

26 Flg Off C. H. Dyson D.F.C., leapt suddenly into the limelight in Egypt when on December 11th 1940 he claimed seven Italian aircraft brought down in one sortie. This exploit led to the award of a Bar for the 33 Squadron pilot's decoration.

27 Mainstay of the R.A.F. over the Desert during the later stages of the First Libyan Campaign was 274 Hurricane Squadron. Seen here in February 1941 are some of the unit's pilots; fourth from left is Flt Lt Wykeham-Barnes; on his left is Sqn Ldr Dunn and then Flt Lt Lapsley; next but one to Lapsley is Flg Off E. M. Mason; all these four officers were ex-members of 80 Squadron.

28 Most unusual in the R.A.F. was the sight of this bearded fighter pilot. Flg Off E. M. 'Imshi' Mason. By the end of January 1941 Mason had in two months claimed over 15 Italian aircraft shot down, being awarded a D.F.C. and becoming R.A.F. top-scorer in the Desert – a position he was not to lose for many months. He was later killed in action on February 15th 1942 while leading 94 Squadron.

29 When the First Libyan Campaign began in December 1940, 3 R.A.A.F. Squadron had just reached the front as an army co-operation unit. On November 19th the squadron fought its first combat when four Gladiators were attacked by a superior force of CR 42s. Although one Gladiator was lost, the others fought back and claimed a number of victories. The three pilots who returned were l. to r. Flg Off A. C. Rawlinson, Flt Lt Pelly and Flg Off A. H. Boyd. Note that the unit's Gladiators at this time carried the code NW, and not the later familiar CV.

30 As British and Empire forces advanced rapidly through the Libyan province of Cyrenaica, captured Italian airfields showed much evidence of the effectiveness of ground strafing attacks by R.A.F. Hurricanes and other aircraft. Here the wreckage of a Fiat CR 42 biplane fighter is being examined.

31 Wreckage of totally destroyed Italian aircraft frames a pair of R.A.F. Hurricanes now operating from this Libyan airfield.

32 Early in the war Malta came under desultory air attack, and in August 1940 Hurricanes were shipped out from Britain aboard the carrier *Argus*, 261 Squadron then being formed on the island. Here are some reinforcement aircraft, received by the squadron later in the year, still fitted with their long-range tanks beneath the wings. The nearest aircraft at least is carrying the rarely-used squadron code, XJ, painted in black on the rear fuselage, and only just visible.

33 The tail of a Fiat CR 42, one of the early victims of Malta's fighter defences.

34 Following the first Hurricanes, a few ex-French contract Martin 167F Maryland 1s were sent to Malta for the vital job of long range reconnaissance. They formed the equipment of 431 Flight at Luqa initially, this being expanded to become 69 Squadron late in 1940 when more aircraft became available.

35 In November 1940 two squadrons of Vickers Wellington 1A bombers flew out to Egypt to join the similarly-equipped 70 Squadron in forming the nucleus of a strategic bombing arm for the R.A.F. in the Mediterranean. 37 Squadron was one of these units, and one of its Wellingtons is here seen in flight low over the Desert.

36 A Wellington of 37 Squadron has a quick wheel-change at a desert airfield in the Nile Delta.

37 Wellingtons of 37 Squadron in Egypt.

38 Late in March 1941 newly-arrived German units under General Erwin Rommel struck at the British forces at El Agheila. These, greatly weakened by the despatch of many units to Greece, crumpled at once, and the British were forced to retreat rapidly back into Egypt. This burnt-out Gladiator was abandoned near Fort Capuzzo on the Libyan border.

39 The first R.A.F. units sent to aid the Greeks, left Egypt in October 1940. Soon in action over the new front were several squadrons of Blenheim 1s, which initially suffered quite severe losses to Italian fighters. Here one of these aircraft of 211 Squadron warms up prior to take off from a Greek airfield.

40 Brought up to strength with Blenheim 1s, 113 Squadron also operated in Greece, several of its aircraft being seen here preparing for a raid.

41 80 Squadron moved to Greece in November 1940, achieving immediate and outstanding success with Gladiator 2s with which it was re-equipped before leaving Africa. In February 1941 Hurricanes began to arrive, and several of the unit's pilots are seen here with one of these; l. to r. Plt Off Dowding, Plt Off Still, Sgt C. E. Casbolt, Wt Off M. Richens, Sgt E. Hewett and Flg Off Flower.

42 In April 1941 German forces attacked Yugoslavia and Greece, and as in the Desert, things swiftly went from bad to worse for the British forces. Shortly before the attack, Sqn Ldr M. T. St. J. Pattle was posted from 80 Squadron to command 33 Squadron, which had also arrived in Greece early in 1941. He is seen here with some of his new squadron; l. to r. Flg Off P. R. W. Wickham, Plt Off Moir, Flt Lt V. C. Woodward, Flg Off Littler, Flg Off E. H. Dean, Flg Off F. Holman, Flg Off Woods, Flg Off Chatham, Plt Off Young, Sqn Ldr Pattle, Flt Lt H. Starrett, Flg Off Rumsey (adj), Flg Off Butcher, Plt Off Winsland and Plt Off Dunscombe.

43 R.A.F. personnel during the retreat through Greece.

44 A detachment of Sunderlands had been based on the Greek coast until April 1941. During the retreat they patrolled between Greece and Crete, protecting Allied shipping, and also evacuated many key personnel.

45 Sunderlands of 228 Squadron off-shore in Western Greece; note the side hatches for lateral defence, through which Vickers K machine guns protrude on these Mark 1s. These were replaced by a dorsal turret on later models.

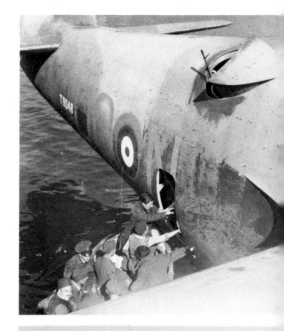

46 R.A.F. evacuees from Greece go aboard a Sunderland of 230 Squadron during April 1941.

47 Not only in Libya and Greece were the British in trouble in April 1941; in Iraq also the situation was threatening as the pro Axis ruler applied pressure on the British. In early May hostilities broke out when the R.A.F. base at Habbaniyah was invested by Iraqi forces, and a relief had to be despatched at once. This force, known as 'Habforce' was supported by a small detachment of Blenheim 4s from 84 and 203 Squadrons, and one of the former unit's aircraft is seen here at a landing ground on the Iraq Transjordan frontier, guarded by Arab Legion sentries.

48 Reinforcements were flown into Habbaniyah, and non-combatants flown out by Bristol Bombay bomber-transports of 216 Squadron from Egypt. These aircraft had undertaken a number of night bombing sorties over targets in Libya during 1940, prior to the arrival of the Wellingtons.

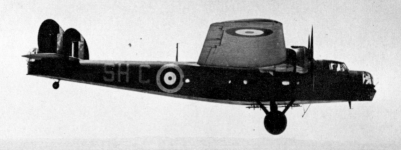

49 Following the pacification of the rising in Iraq, it became necessary to neutralise the hostile Vichy French colony of Syria. A force was assembled and an invasion was begun on June 8th 1941. To gain air superiority in the area the new Curtiss Tomahawk fighters of 3 R.A.A.F. Squadron were allocated. These aircraft had only just arrived from America, and the Syrian campaign was to be their first serious test.

50 Lined up ready to go are Tomahawks of 3 R.A.A.F. Squadron on an airfield in Palestine near the Syrian border.

51 Flying over the craggy landscape of Syria, 3 R.A.A.F. Squadron's Tomahawks proved markedly successful; they rapidly attained a degree of superiority over the fighters of the Armee de l'Air, and on several occasions dealt savagely with enemy bomber formations.

52 The Syrian campaign saw the last front line use of the Lysander in the Mediterranean area. Here an aircraft of 208 Squadron wings its way over the city of Beirut, following its capture. Lysanders operated with one flight of 208 Squadron at this time, the other two flights using Hurricanes.

53 In May 1941 the major area of concern to the British was Crete. As forces in Greece began to retreat to this island, a fighter squadron of the Royal Navy No 805, which had been based in Egypt on coastal patrol duties, was despatched to the island to assist the R.A.F. in its defence, taking with it a mixed bag of Sea Gladiators, Fairey Fulmars, and Brewster Buffalos, one of which is seen here in a hangar in Egypt. These aircraft were all swiftly destroyed on the ground.

54 During the later stages of the fighting on Crete, following the German airborne landings there, long-range Hurricanes from Egypt operated over the island. Probably the most successful of the pilots so engaged was Flt Lt D. S. G. Honor, of 274 Squadron, who shot down four aircraft and destroyed two more on the ground in three sorties. On the third he was brought down himself by a Messerschmitt Bf 109, and baled out into the sea, swimming ashore. He remained on the island for six days, finally being picked up by a Sunderland flyingboat.

55 The activities over Crete late in May by aircraft from Egypt, saw the operational debut in this area of the Martin Maryland as a bomber, and also as a long range fighter, aircraft of 24 S.A.A.F. Squadron, newly-arrived from East Africa, co-operating with Hurricanes on these duties.

56 Another view of Maryland 1680 of 24 S.A.A.F. Squadron in May 1941.

57 Maryland 1663 'W' is prepared for a sortie in June 1941. During that month a limited offensive was launched in the Western Desert under the codename Operation 'Battleaxe'; it was a disastrous failure.

58 A South African Maryland 2 about to take off from a Desert landing ground. Note that two guns were fitted in the turret.

59 Having formed up, the Marylands set off on their raid. The number of aircraft in this formation indicates that two squadrons are taking part — probably 12 S.A.A.F. and 24 S.A.A.F. Squadrons. Four of the bombers are still painted in standard R.A.F. green/brown camouflage, while the other dozen have been repainted brown and stone, an indication that this photograph was probably taken during the early summer of 1941.

60 Another new South African unit to arrive in Egypt from East Africa in May 1941 was 1 S.A.A.F. Squadron, soon to play a major part in the Desert air fighting. Here three of the squadron's Hurricanes take the air, followed by a further pair.

61 The conclusion of the campaigns in Greece, Crete and Iraq, and the end of the main fighting in East Africa, allowed the number of squadrons of Blenheim 4s in Egypt to be substantially increased during the summer of 1941. Here one of these aircraft, newly painted in brown and stone, flies low over the Desert.

62 During May 1941 the aircraft carrier H.M.S. *Furious* carried Hurricanes and pilots from 213, 229 and 238 Squadrons out to the Mediterranean, where they took off and flew to Egypt via Malta. The pilots of the two former units were attached to 73 and 274 Squadrons for a short while, before forming fully into squadrons again with the arrival by sea of their ground echelons.

63 After fully re-forming during the summer of 1941, 213 Squadron was despatched to Cyprus to provide the air defence of that island. A line of the unit's Hurricanes are seen here at Nicosia soon after their arrival. It will be noted that several of these fighters have not yet been fitted with tropical filters beneath their noses.

64 While on a training flight at Nicosia, Flg Off Wallace of 213 Squadron flipped this non-tropicalised Hurricane on to its back while landing; this was Flg Off Wallace's seventh 'prang'!

65 213 Squadron gradually received fully tropicalised Hurricanes, and this one, an aircraft of 'B' Flight, seen here taxiing down the Nicosia runway, has also had the underside of the nose and the leading edges of the wings painted with 'snake'-type camouflage, designed to distract anti-aircraft gunners during low level strafes.

66 After its success in Syria, 3 R.A.A.F. Squadron was soon back in the Western Desert, where the Tomahawk had already entered action with 250 Squadron. Here 'B' Flight of the squadron display their battle honours as they prepare to return to the front.

67 Tomahawk 2B of 3 R.A.A.F. Squadron shows well its lines as it enters a climbing turn.

68 Silhouetted against the sun, Tomahawk 'R' of 3 R.A.A.F. Squadron shows its distinctive shape well in this photograph. Against the Messerschmitts in the Desert, the Tomahawks had a much tougher fight than they had previously encountered with the French Dewoitine fighters in Syria.

69 The Tomahawk packed quite a heavy punch, particularly from the pair of .50in Browning machine guns mounted above the engine. It proved a most competent bomber destroyer, and this head-on view of a 3 R.A.A.F. Squadron aircraft must have been the last thing seen by a number of German and Italian rear gunners.

70 On September 24th 1941 2nd Lt MacRobert of 1 S.A.A.F. Squadron (left) was shot down by a Bf 109E of I/JG 27. Lt Liebenberg (right), having damaged one of the attacking Messerschmitts, landed alongside the shattered Hurricane which MacRobert had crash-landed, and packing the pilot into the cockpit of his own Hurricane, climbed on to his knees and took off again to fly back to base. Rescues of this sort were to become relatively common during the fighting in North Africa, where safe landings on the open Desert could often be made.

71 The fourth squadron of Tomahawks to join the units at the front in Egypt was 112 Squadron, re-equipped since its stirring days in Greece and Crete. This was the first unit to paint 'shark's teeth' on its Curtiss fighters — a practice later followed by the P-40 pilots of several nations. This group of pilots are seen with one of their aircraft in November 1941, just before the great offensive known as Operation 'Crusader' was launched. L. to r. (standing) Sgt R. M. Leu, Plt Off N. F. Duke, Flg Off Soden, Flg Off Humphreys, Sqn Ldr A. Morello, Flt Lt Ambrose, Flg Off Dickinson, Sgt Burney, and Flg Off D. F. Westenra; (squatting) Flg Off J. J. P. Sabourin, Flg Off N. Bowker, Flg Off J. P. Bartle and Sgt Carson.

72 Throughout the campaigns in the Mediterranean during 1941 and 1942, the Short Sunderland flyingboats of 230 Squadron continued to operate on long range sea reconnaissance and vital transport missions. Here one of the squadron's aircraft is seen taking off near Alexandria.

73 With the fall of Yugoslavia in April 1941, a number of aircraft of the Yugoslav Army and Naval Air Forces escaped to Egypt. Several of these were Dornier Do 22 floatplanes, and these, together with their crews, joined one flight of 230 Squadron at Alexandria, retaining their Yugoslav national markings, and operating alongside the unit's Sunderlands for many months.

74 During 1941 all tactical reconnaissance over the front was undertaken by Hurricanes, usually operating in pairs. Here one of these aircraft, carrying the name 'Olive II' beneath the cockpit, is seen in flight; in the background, the defending 'weaver' can just be seen. It is believed that these are aircraft of 237 (Rhodesian) Squadron.

75 To join the R.A.F. in nocturnal missions, Royal Navy Fairey Albacore torpedo bombers of 826 Squadron operated from Desert airfields for many months. They undertook torpedo attacks on Axis shipping between Africa and Europe, and also accompanied Wellingtons on bombing raids, illuminating the target areas with flares for these latter aircraft. Here one of these Albacores is seen being fitted with a torpedo.

76 Three Royal Navy Albacores fly along the coast, just inland from the sea. These aircraft are carrying flares beneath their wings.

77 Malta had suffered its first serious aerial onslaught following the arrival of the Luftwaffe in the Mediterranean, and had been fighting for survival during the early months of 1941. Here a bomb is seen exploding on the island during an attack on one of the airfields.

78 The concentrated German air attack on Malta took a heavy toll of aircraft on the ground. Here one of 69 Squadron's Marylands has been shattered by a bomb while standing unprotected on the open airfield at Luqa.

79 Malta's limestone was easily cut, and soon hardened into an adequate defence when exposed to the air. The Luftwaffe's attacks led to the urgent construction of blast pens for aircraft, like this one being built by Army personnel.

80 The anti-aircraft defences of Malta were always heavy, and all personnel were encouraged to fire on enemy aircraft during attacks. Here a pair of Vickers 'K' machine guns have been mounted to assist in airfield defence.

81 Safe from all but a direct hit in its limestone and sandbag blast pen, this Hurricane is readied for action from Malta as its Flt Sgt pilot settles himself into his cockpit, aided by one of the ground crew.

82 In the early summer of 1941 the Luftwaffe left Sicily, and Malta was developed as a major offensive base to attack shipping carrying supplies and reinforcements to the Axis armies in Africa. Squadrons of Blenheim 4s from Bomber Command's 2 Group in England were sent out to the island on detachment to undertake low-flying anti-shipping duties, and here a quartette of these aircraft from 21 Squadron are seen on such a mission near Linosa Island.

83 In the Desert, long-range strategic reconnaissance was undertaken during the latter part of 1941 by Maryland 1s of 60 S.A.A.F. Squadron. Here one of these aircraft is having its camera checked before take-off. Note that on this aircraft turret armament is only a single Vickers K gun.

84 Bombs being taken out to South African Marylands as the R.A.F. begins the pre-offensive softening-up of Axis targets in November 1941.

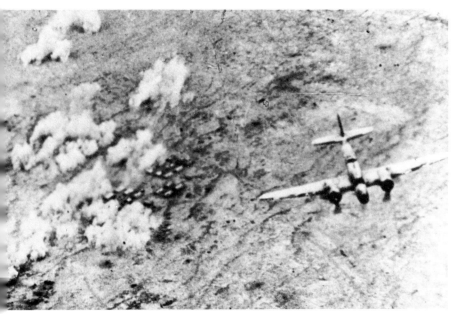

85 Bombs from South African Marylands bursting on an Axis vehicle concentration in the Desert late in 1941.

86 For Operation 'Crusader' a Free French unit, the 'Lorraine' Squadron, joined the R.A.F., its aircraft carrying not only roundels and French-style rudder striping, but also Cross of Lorraine markings both on fuselage and wings. Here three of the unit's Blenheim 4s are seen in formation.

87 A Free French 'Lorraine' Squadron Blenheim 4 shows well its colourful and unusual markings.

88 For Operation 'Crusader' the R.A.F. disposed seven squadrons and a detachment of Blenheim 4s for operations over the front. One of these aircraft shows well the asymetric nose geometry of this model.

89 When caught without fighter escort, the Blenheim was a relatively vulnerable aircraft, and on occasions suffered heavy losses. This particular aircraft has crash-landed on an enemy airfield during an attack, and has burnt out.

90 Blenheim 4s on a Desert landing ground at dusk. One aircraft comes in to land, while that in the foreground has been shrouded for the night.

91 At the start of Operation 'Crusader' in late November 1941, one of the three South African Maryland squadrons, 24 S.A.A.F., had replaced these aircraft with the first examples of a new American light bomber to arrive in Africa, the Douglas Boston 3. One of these aircraft is seen here over Egypt during an early test flight.

92 A Boston 3 of 24 S.A.A.F. Squadron, being prepared for action. The fairing covering the pair of forward-firing machine guns on the port side of the aircraft has been removed so that the guns may be armed.

93 Among the American aircraft reaching Africa in ever-growing numbers were Lockheed Lodestar transports. Here is an ambulance conversion of one of these, operated by an Air Ambulance Flight of the S.A.A.F.

94 By late 1941 five squadrons of Tomahawks were operational in the Desert, two of these being S.A.A.F. units. Here three South African Tomahawk 2Bs are seen taking off from a forward landing ground.

95 The Curtiss Kittyhawk was developed from the earlier Tomahawk, and incorporated an increased armament of six wing-mounted .50in guns. The first aircraft arrived in Egypt too late to be in service for the start of Operation 'Crusader', but as the British advance across Cyrenaica reached its end, the first of several squadrons were withdrawn late in December to replace Tomahawks with these aircraft. Several of the new aircraft, some still in brown/green delivery camouflage, are seen at a maintenance unit in Egypt awaiting issue to squadrons. In the background is a Hurricane.

96 A formation of four of the new Kittyhawk 1 fighters is flown as pilots familiarise themselves with the new aircraft.

97 Into action; newly-arrived Kittyhawks escort a formation of Blenheim 4s over the front early in 1942.

98 Five squadrons of Wellingtons were available during the 'Crusader' operations, being used mainly to attack Axis supply ports at Benghazi and Tripoli. It is noteworthy that this particular aircraft has had its black underside repainted in a lighter shade for day operations.

99 Losses of Hurricanes during late 1941, and 1942 were very heavy. The R.A.F. Repair and Salvage organisation scoured the Desert for repairable crashed aircraft with remarkable efficiency, bringing back literally hundreds of aircraft on its 'Queen Marys'. The repair organisation supplemented the delivery of new aircraft to a quite remarkable degree.

100 1 S.A.A.F. Squadron remained one of the most successful Hurricane units at the front from May 1941 to November 1942, although suffering very heavy losses. Here several of the unit's aircraft prepare to take off. Note the very roughly applied 'S' on Z5469.

101 Bristol Beaufighters were introduced to Desert service in May 1941, and when Operation 'Crusader' began, two squadrons were available. After many strafing attacks on Axis convoys and camps during the summer of 1941, they played a vital part in the opening days of the offensive with a series of surprise attacks on enemy airfields, during which they destroyed a substantial number of aircraft on the ground.

102 Carrying a quite devastating forward-firing armament of four 20mm cannons and six .303in machine guns, the Beaufighter could do terrific damage. Here one takes off from its base at Edcu; three more can be seen dispersed in the background. Initial operations with these aircraft in the Mediterranean area were flown by 252 and 272 Squadrons.

103 Despite a catastrophic mission on December 10th 1941 when five of six Bostons of 24 S.A.A.F. Squadron were shot down by fighters after being caught over the front without an escort, the new bombers were finding their feet by the turn of the year, and 12 S.A.A.F. Squadron also withdrew to convert to the aircraft. Here Bostons of 24 S.A.A.F. Squadron are seen running up their engines prior to take off.

104 A flight of Boston 3s of 12 S.A.A.F. Squadron wings over the Desert. After initial losses, the aircraft were never again sent out without adequate fighter escort. When escorted, their precision bombing attacks quickly increased in accuracy to a marked degree.

105 Bristol Beaufort 2 torpedo-bombers were another new addition to air strength in the Mediterranean early in 1942. 22 Squadron flew out from England to Egypt, via Malta, while more of these aircraft were delivered by the ferry route to replace 39 Squadron's Marylands.

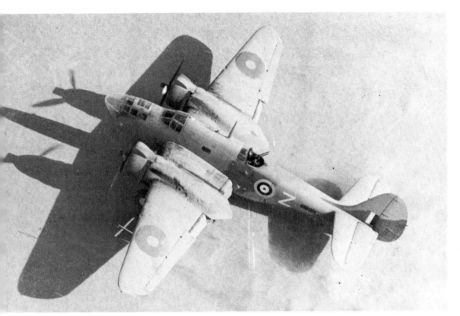

106 A third new bomber to make its Desert debut was the Martin Baltimore, developed from the Maryland. Following the delivery of a few Mark 1s, Mark 2s first went into action with 223 Squadron during May. Like the Bostons, they went out unescorted and were cut to pieces, the rear armament proving unsatisfactory. Once modified, and with proper escort, they joined the Bostons in many successful raids.

107 Second squadron to take the Baltimore 2 into action was 55 Squadron, and an aircraft of this unit is seen here. Note that the wing-mounted forward-firing armament can be clearly distinguished in this view. One further squadron was to receive Baltimores during the year, this being 21 S.A.A.F. Squadron, the third of the South African light bomber units.

108 A pair of Baltimore 2s of 55 Squadron on a Desert airfield during the early summer of 1942.

109 The Americans were now in the war, and early in 1942 President Roosevelt flew to meet Winston Churchill at Cairo to discuss the position. Here his specially modified B-24 bomber is seen taxiing in on arrival. Note the Meteorological Flight Gladiator in the near background, and the Wellington in the far left distance.

110 This rather dim photograph is of peculiar interest in that it depicts a pair of Hurricanes of an unidentified unit over the Desert. The nearer aircraft also appears to have a coat of arms painted beneath the cockpit. It is possible that the aircraft may be of 127 Squadron.

111 Hurricane 2Bs of 1 S.A.A.F. Squadron on a Desert airfield.

112 A pair of Hurricane 2s of 213 Squadron (AK-W and AK-I) escort a
V.I.P.-carrying Lockheed Lodestar of 267 Squadron (KW-V) over Egyptian territory.

113 The South African Prime Minister, General Jan Smuts, arrives in a Lodestar
to inspect South African units in the Desert.

114 A renewed Luftwaffe 'Blitz' on Malta during early 1942 led to the despatch to the island during March of the first Spitfires to leave the United Kingdom (other than a few unarmed reconnaissance machines). Here a Spitfire 5 is seen being rearmed in a typical Malta blast pen.

115 Soon after the arrival of Spitfires on Malta, command of the island's air defences was taken over by Air Vice-Marshal Sir Keith Park. He is seen here in the back seat of an M.G. tourer while inspecting the airfields. In the background is a Spitfire 5 in a sandbagged pen.

116 The first radar-equipped night fighters arrived in Egypt in 1942 with 89 Squadron from England. Soon after their initial sorties, one flight was despatched to Malta, and it was here that this early all-black Beaufighter N.F.1 is seen.

117 69 Squadron at Luqa, Malta, also gained some new aircraft during mid 1942 with the arrival of a few Baltimore 1s and 2s to supplement its Marylands and Hurricanes.

118 By the summer of 1942 Malta's defences were becoming much more formidable. In this typical scene, a Beaufighter of one of the strike squadrons comes in to land past three Spitfire 5s of 249 Squadron.

119 Spitfires for the Desert were not far behind those for Malta, though initially they arrived only in very small numbers. First squadron to arrive in Egypt from England with these aircraft was 145, two aircraft of this unit being seen here. They first went into action in June, during Rommel's offensive on the Gazala Line.

120 Although only available initially in very small numbers, the arrival of the Spitfire 5s gave the pilots of the Kittyhawks, Tomahawks and Hurricanes in the Desert a welcome degree of relief from the attacks of the high-flying Bf 109Fs, which were now faced with a more formidable adversary. A 145 Squadron Spitfire prepares for take off.

121 For several years 202 Squadron at Gibraltar undertook the thankless task of anti-submarine and convoy escort patrol over the Western Mediterranean, and the Atlantic approaches. For most of that time the squadron operated Consolidated Catalina flyingboats, one of which is seen here, carrying depth charges beneath its wings.

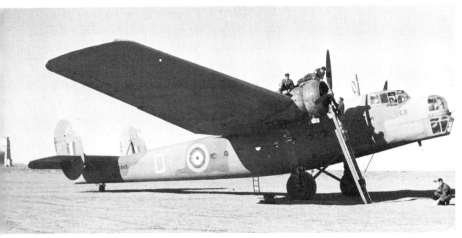

122 Throughout all the campaigns in the Western Desert, 216 Squadron continued to operate its faithful Bristol Bombays. One is seen here during 1942, near an Italian monument, erected in the Desert of Libya.

123 Another aircraft which gave long and useful service in Egypt and Libya was the De Havilland DH.86A. A number of these aircraft served with 1 R.A.A.F. Air Ambulance Unit on casualty evacuation duties. At least one of these aircraft was shot down by an intruding Messerschmitt Bf 110. Note that this aircraft is carrying the Australian serial, A31-7.

124 For aircraft operating over the sea, an embryo Air/Sea Rescue Service was gradually growing in size during 1942. One of the main types used was the Vickers Walrus amphibian, and one of these aircraft of a Royal Navy unit is seen here over the sea at this time.

125 A small number of these Fairchild 91 amphibians were put into service by the R.A.F. for air/sea rescue, flying from the Alexandria area.

126 A Wellington co-operates with an R.A.F. High-Speed Launch on air/sea rescue duties in the Mediterranean during 1942.

127 In June 1942 213 Squadron moved into Libya to take part in operations over the front. As one of the pilots leaves his Hurricane 2C at Gambut, he is met by Sqn Ldr M. H. Young and Flt Lt G. H. Westlake.

128 The mid-1942 fighting at Gazala was the last occasion in which the Tomahawk played a really major part in the air. Serving with two squadrons of 233 Wing, 4 S.A.A.F. and 5 S.A.A.F., and also with flights of two tactical reconnaissance units, their losses at this time were very heavy. Here a Tomahawk of 4 S.A.A.F. Squadron prepares to take off.

129 'Chakka', a Tomahawk of 5 S.A.A.F. Squadron in summer 1942.

130 S.A.A.F. Tomahawks frequently carried ornamentation and names during 1942; this one has a relatively simple painting of a Red Indian, wearing a South African bush shirt, and brandishing (of course) a tomahawk.

131 A much more elaborate design embellishes the cowling of this S.A.A.F. Tomahawk, which also sports a name.

132 With two names is Lt Kemsley's Tomahawk of 5 S.A.A.F. Squadron.

133 233 Wing at an airfield in the Gazala area in May 1942. In the foreground is Kittyhawk DB-P of 2 S.A.A.F. Squadron; in the background are Tomahawks of 4 S.A.A.F. Squadron, including KJ-K, and further 2 S.A.A.F. Squadron Kittyhawks.

134 During the Gazala fighting the Kittyhawks, which could carry initially up to 500 lbs. of bombs (which the Tomahawk could not) first went fully into action as fighter-bombers. Here GA-C of 112 Squadron takes off carrying a single 250 lb. bomb, to attack Axis armoured columns.

135 Bomb-carrying Kittyhawks of 3 R.A.A.F. Squadron, ready for action on a Desert landing ground.

136 One of the most successful exponents of the Kittyhawk as a fighter was Plt Off J. L. Waddy, an Australian, who gained 12½ victories flying these aircraft. He is seen here in an aircraft of 250 Squadron carrying the name Ve, after his wife.

137 Several new squadrons were formed in Egypt during 1942, and one of these was 335, the first Greek fighter squadron in the R.A.F. Here one of the unit's Hurricanes, pristine new, and without tropical filter, is seen returning from a training flight.

138 On return from a sortie over the front, the pilot of a tactical reconnaissance Hurricane discusses his observations with an Army liaison officer. Note the pad strapped to the pilot's right knee.

139 A Wellington takes off from the Delta for another mission against Benghazi as Rommel's Afrika Korps forces the British Army into retreat from Gazala.

140 With the crisis situation in the Desert in mid 1942, several detachments of Handley-Page Halifax 1 heavy bombers were rushed out to the Desert to join the Wellingtons in the night offensive. These were initially formed into two composite squadrons, and here one of these aircraft sets out on a raid before night falls.

141 Other heavy bombers, this time American-built Consolidated Liberator 2s of 160 Squadron, were on their way through the Mediterranean to India in mid 1942, and were retained in Egypt to assist the Wellingtons and Halifaxes.

142 Halifax 1 about to leave on a night bombing mission from a base in the Nile Delta.

143 By the time the forces on the ground had established themselves on the line at El Alamein late in July 1942, the first examples of the Baltimore 3 were arriving with the squadrons. These aircraft carried the more effective rear defence of four .303in machine guns in a Boulton-Paul hydraulically operated turret. The four guns can just be seen on this Baltimore 3 as it turns for home after bombing enemy concentrations in the Desert.

144 Another view of a Baltimore 3, taken somewhat later in 1942, shows to good advantage the four-gun turret.

145 A Baltimore of 232 Wing takes off, passing over another still on the airfield.

146 South African Boston 3 of 3 S.A.A.F. Wing is given the 'thumbs up' for take off during September 1942, as Rommel's forces attack the Alamein Line at Alam el Halfa.

147 South African Bostons taking off; the nearest aircraft has just left the ground, as has that in the right distance. Four others have already got their wheels retracted as they set course for their objective.

148 Undergoing major servicing is this South African Boston 3. Note the airscrew on the oil drum in the foreground; the port aileron has also been removed.

149 Beaufighters in the Mediterranean area rarely carried squadron codes, but this Mark 1C, T4767, serving with 252 Squadron at Edcu in mid 1942 is carrying the code BT-T. BT has not previously been listed as 252 Squadron's code.

150 An unusual sight at Edcu was this Blenheim 4 'hack' aircraft of 89 night-fighter Squadron, which painted the aircraft with its unusual 'face'. Instead of an individual identification letter, it carried a '?'.

151 In August 1942 the surviving Beauforts of two squadrons which had flown out to the Mediterranean from England, 86 and 217, and 39 Squadron in Egypt, were amalgamated to form a new 39 Squadron. Here one of this unit's aircraft, still wearing the codes of 86 Squadron, attacks an Axis tanker in the Ionian Sea on September 15th 1942.

152 Kittyhawk 1 of 3 R.A.A.F. Squadron, CV-J, AK581, is examined by salvage personnel.

153 As the Axis armoured columns approached the Alamein Line in summer 1942, the R.A.F. introduced a new weapon to the front, the 'tank-buster'. The first such unit was 6 Squadron, which now operated Hurricane 2Ds, each carrying a pair of 40mm anti-tank guns beneath the wings. Four of the squadron's aircraft are seen here in flight.

154 A South African Kittyhawk of 233 Wing displays an unusual crest on its nose.

155 The crews of strike Beaufighters being delivered to their dispersed aircraft by lorry. The Beaufighter, marked with three victory tallies on the nose, is believed to be an aircraft of 252 Squadron.

156 During 1942 increasing numbers of Lockheed Hudsons converted for the transport role, were becoming available to the transport squadrons in Egypt. This aircraft is a converted Mark 1. Note the fairing on the top of the rear fuselage where the turret has been removed. Note also the Liberator bomber immediately to the rear.

157 A flight of Hurricanes of 94 Squadron; this unit was on air defence duties in the Alexandria area. Note that these aircraft, Mark 2Cs, have all had two of the four 20mm cannons removed to improve the aircraft's performance.

158 Increasing numbers of Spitfires available on Malta during the summer of 1942 were making Axis attacks on the island progressively more expensive. Here Spitfires are overhauled and repaired in a workshop on the island.

159 A Malta Spitfire begins its take off run during the late summer of 1942. Note that the new style of R.A.F. roundel introduced at this time, has been painted on this aircraft.

160 The successful pilot of an 89 Squadron Beaufighter on Malta points out his score tally to an admiring ground crew. Note that the brown and stone upper surface camouflage has been painted directly over the previous all-black finish, leaving only the undersides black. The aircraft's name, 'Young Hunter III', has been carefully painted round. It is believed that the pilot was Flg Off R. C. Fumerton, D.F.C., a Canadian member of the unit.

161 Interested Maltese watch as
R.A.F. personnel examine a
Macchi 202 fighter shot down
by Flg Off G. F. Beurling of 249
Squadron on Malta.

162 Flg Off G. F. Beurling,
D.F.M., with trophies from the
Macchi shot down by him.
Beurling was the most successful
fighter pilot on Malta, claiming
$26\frac{1}{3}$ victories during the summer
of 1942. He eventually received
a D.S.O., D.F.C., and a Bar to his
D.F.M.

163 A pair of Spitfires over Malta in the early autumn of 1942. T-B is an aircraft of 249 Squadron; F-A is believed to belong to 229 Squadron.

164 Following the Battle of El Alamein in October/November 1942, the R.A.F. was able once more to move forward towards Libya; a Hurricane has arrived on a landing ground recently occupied by the Luftwaffe, and interested pilots are examining the remains of a Messerschmitt Bf 110 of ZG 26.

165 Troops of the 51st Highland Division prepare to go aboard Hudson 6 transports of 117 Squadron to be flown up to the front.

166 On November 13th 1942 Hudson 6s of 117 Squadron flew servicing personnel and supplies of 243 Wing forward to Landing Ground 125, deep in the Cyrenaican Desert, behind enemy lines. Four of the unit's Hudsons are seen here in flight; they carry the codes LO.

167 At LG 125 Hurricanes of 213 and 238 Squadrons arrive to undertake several days of strafing attacks on enemy columns far behind the lines. The Axis were at a loss to know where the Hurricanes could have suddenly appeared from. A Hurricane 2C of 213 Squadron and a Hudson 6 transport of 117 Squadron are seen here at the secret landing ground.

168 On November 8th 1942, with the Alamein battle just won, British and American troops landed in French North Africa. R.A.F. units moved swiftly into Algeria, and Spitfires are seen here at Maison Blanche shortly after arrival. In the left foreground is the nose of a Hurricane of 43 Squadron.

169 Bombs are delivered for a Hurricane 2C in Algeria, as the British 1st Army moves quickly towards western Tunisia. This Hurricane is believed to be an aircraft of 241 Army Co-Operation Squadron.

170 Spitfire 5s of 154 Squadron, one of the first squadrons to fly over to North Africa from Gibraltar following the initial landings. This unit moved forward to defend the small port of Bougie as the advance into Tunisia progressed.

171 Three squadrons of Beaufighter night fighters were flown out to Algeria early in the fighting, but with the radar removed for security purposes before they left, they were almost helpless on arrival. Once radar sets were flown out to them, they quickly took a heavy toll of Axis bombers over Algiers, Bougie and Bone.

172 Spitfire 5 in North Africa.

173 With the winter of 1942 came the most appalling bad weather for many years in French North Africa. In Tunisia the Army and the R.A.F. were soon bogged down, and in the Algiers area, the overcrowded airfields were soon morasses. Here 32 Squadron Hurricanes of 323 Wing, some in brown and stone, others in green and grey camouflage, share a dispersal with a B-25 Mitchell bomber of the U.S.A.A.F.

174 500lb bombs being brought up for Kittyhawk 3 fighter-bombers of 260 Squadron at an airfield to the east of Tripoli. By early 1943 260 Squadron had joined 239 Wing, 233 Wing becoming 7 S.A.A.F. Wing. The Desert Air Force and the 8th Army were now approaching Tunisia from the south.

175 Sqn Ldr R. H. M. Gibbes, commanding officer of 3 R.A.A.F. Squadron with the explicit cartoon painted on the nose of his Kittyhawk.

176 Damaged Kittyhawks are repaired at a forward maintenance base. Note the badly bent airscrew of the aircraft in the foreground, the set of wings immediately behind this, and the wingless Kittyhawk 1 of 4 S.A.A.F. Squadron to the rear.

177 Kittyhawk 3 of 250 Squadron, 239 Wing, in early 1943. This is FR291; note that the cowling shroud is marked with the aircraft's full identification letters, LD-A.

178 Wounded troops await air transport early in 1943. In the foreground is the nose of a 216 Squadron Bombay with a tasteful piece of artwork beneath the cockpit. Beyond the troops, the tail can just be seen of a B.O.A.C. Lodestar.

179 Humber armoured cars of an
R.A.F. Armoured Car Company,
on a North African airfield;
behind them are two Hudson 6
transports.

180 A Spitfire pilot of 145
Squadron discusses the situation
with a Naval pilot at an airfield in
Tripolitania in January 1943.
Note the rather exotic code
letters now applied to 145
Squadron's Spitfires in the
background.

181 One of the more successful Spitfire pilots of 244 Wing during the fighting in the Desert was Flt Lt W. L. Chisholm, a Canadian pilot with 92 Squadron. Early in 1943 he had six victories to his credit, and was soon to be awarded both a D.F.C. and a Bar to this; by time the the fighting in Tunisia ended his score had risen to eight.

182 Prior to moving forward into Tripolitania for operations over the Mareth Line, Bostons of 12 S.A.A.F. Squadron fly over Cairo.

183 As the Desert Air Force's assault on the Mareth defences gets underway in early March 1943, a Baltimore of 232 Wing prepares to undertake a sortie over this target. The aircraft is a Mark 3A, the first model to be supplied under Lend Lease. It differs from the Mark 3 in having a Martin electrically-operated dorsal turret mounting a pair of .50in Browning machine guns.

184 As the early morning sun rises above the horizon, Bostons of 3 S.A.A.F. Wing flood into the sky to hammer the Mareth Line once more.

185 From their bases far back in Egypt, the Wellingtons of 205 Group were as active as ever during the build-up to the Mareth battle. Here 500lb bombs are being taken out to the waiting aircraft – in this case Merlin-engined Mark 2s.

186 By late 1943 all the various Halifax detachments had been amalgamated into 462 Squadron, nominally at least an R.A.A.F. unit. Here one of the squadron's Halifax 1s flies out towards the looming dusk on its way towards the Tunisian border.

187 On a scrub-covered Libyan airfield, a Boston of 3 S.A.A.F. Wing prepares for action. This is not a British contract Boston, but an American A-20 Havoc, taken over from the U.S.A.A.F., and still carrying its American service serial on its fin.

188 The Baltimore was a tough aircraft; a Mark 3A of 232 Wing flies back to base in Tripolitania after an attack on Mareth, the top half of its rudder shot clean away by a flak burst. Note the more varied scenery below, quite a change after the flat and featureless desert.

189 Wing Leader of 244 Squadron in early 1943 was Wg Cdr I. R. Gleed, D.F.C., seen here flying his personal clipped-wing Spitfire 5, IR-G, carrying his 'Figaro' mascot beneath the cockpit. A most notable fighter pilot and leader, Wg Cdr Gleed was shot down and killed on April 16th 1943 in a fight with Bf 109Gs of JG 77, while leading an attack on a formation of Axis transport aircraft; he had at least 13 victories to his credit at the time of his death.

190 A Beaufighter of 252 Squadron in Libya. 272 Squadron moved to Malta in November 1942 to take part in operations over Northern Tunisia, and 252 remained as the only strike Beaufighter unit with Desert Air Force. Its aircraft continued to punish Axis columns and coastal shipping until after the Mareth Line battle, when the squadron fell back into Egypt to operate over the Aegean Sea.

191 Early in March 1943, just before the Mareth battle began, a unit of experienced volunteer Polish fighter pilots, the Polish Fighting Team, was attached to 145 Squadron of 244 Wing for operations, and a number of Spitfire 9s were supplied to this unit, mainly for their use. Several of these aircraft, marked with the Polish national marking ahead of the cockpits, are seen here. To differentiate them from the rest of 145 Squadron, while the squadron aircraft carried individual letters, those of the Polish team carried numbers. ZX-6, the nearest aircraft, is flown by Sqn Ldr S. F. Skalski, who led the Poles in the air.

192 Late in the Tunisian campaign, 152 Squadron became the first official Spitbomber fighter-bomber squadron, carrying a 250lb bomb beneath each wing of its Spitfire 5s. Here is an experimental fitting of one such bomb to an aircraft of this sort.

193 Early in the Tunisian fighting, four squadrons of Bristol Bisley bombers had operated by day, but had suffered appalling losses, and had been relegated to night operations. In April 1943 two of these squadrons, 18 and 114, forming part of 326 Wing, at last received some Boston 3s just in time for the final push on Tunis and Bizerta. One of these latter aircraft is seen here over the Tunisian countryside.

194 Halifax 1s of 462 Squadron show well the effect of exhaust gases and African sand to their paintwork. By April 1943 the heavy bombers of 205 Group were beginning to reach further afield, towards targets in Southern Europe, as the war in Tunisia drew inexorably to a close.

195 The first De Havilland Mosquitos to operate in the Mediterranean area were a few photo-reconnaissance aircraft sent to 60 S.A.A.F. Squadron in Libya early in 1943, and the intruder Mark 2s of 23 Squadron, one of which is seen here over Malta. The squadron arrived from England to undertake night intruding sorties over Sicilian airfields, led by Wg Cdr P. G. Wykeham-Barnes.

196 Beaufighter 1s of 272 Squadron on Malta, which scoured the sea between Sicily and Tunisia, strafing and bombing Axis shipping attempting to supply the beleaguered forces there, and also took a heavy toll of the transport aircraft used in vast numbers on this route. Note the bomb racks beneath the wings, and the Vickers 'K' gun in the navigator's hatch. These were carried regularly from late 1942, and were frequently used for rear defence.

197 14 Squadron had been the last unit to operate Blenheim 4s over the Desert. Withdrawn in the late summer of 1942, it returned to operations in the Spring of 1943 with Martin Marauder 1 bombers. Fitted for torpedo-carrying, and used for anti-shipping attacks and reconnaissances, they moved from Tripolitania to Blida on the Algerian coast just before the fall of the last Axis forces in Tunisia. Three of the squadron's aircraft are seen here over North Africa.